The Prentice Hall Mini-Series in Music ... proach to equipping all teachers for success in the music classroom ... provides succinctly written texts covering the information needed, first, to qualify for teacher certification in music education, and second, to adapt to the increasingly broad and diverse demands placed on the teacher in today's schools. A third focus of the series is to enable the teacher in the classroom to appropriately integrate music with other instruction in ways that support the teaching specialist to reach the objectives of music teaching and learning. The range of topics in the series emphasizes the goals of a valid music program, beginning with pre-kindergarten, a program that is varied and flexible without sacrificing competence in musical skills, understanding, and knowledge.

Musical Lives
of Young Children

John W. Flohr

PEARSON

Prentice
Hall

Upper Saddle River, NJ 07458

Library of Congress Cataloging-in-Publication Data

Flohr, John W.
  Musical lives of young children / John W. Flohr.
      p. cm.
    Includes bibliographical references (p.) and index.
    ISBN 0-13-048694-9
    1. Music—Instruction and study—Juvenile.   I. Title.

  MT1.F54 2004
  372.87—dc21

2003056540

VP, Editorial Director: Charlyce Jones Owen
Senior Acquisitions Editor: Christopher T. Johnson
Editorial Assistant: Evette Dickerson
Marketing Manager: Sheryl Adams
Marketing Assistant: Kimberly Daum
Managing Editor: Joanne Riker
Production Editor: Laura A. Lawrie
Manufacturing and Prepress Buyer: Benjamin D. Smith
Cover Designer: Bruce Kenselaar
Composition: This book was set in 10/12 Times by Stratford Publishing Services
Printer/Binder: Interior printed by Phoenix Book Tech. The cover was printed by Lehigh Press

Credits and acknowledgments borrowed from other sources and reproduced, with permission, in this textbook appear on appropriate page within text.

Pearson Education LTD.   Pearson Education Australia PTY, Limited
Pearson Education Singapore, Pte. Ltd   Pearson Education North Asia Ltd
Pearson Education, Canada, Ltd   Pearson Educación de Mexico, S.A. de C.V.
Pearson Education-Japan   Pearson Education Malaysia, Pte. Ltd

10 9 8 7 6 5 4 3 2 1
ISBN 0-13-048694-9

Contents

Preface

I began writing this book because of my belief that the nurturing of children's musical interest is of great import to children's development and their emotional lives. Teachers and parents around the world observe children's joyful affinity for music.

The challenge in writing a mini-series book about the large subject of music for young children was deciding what to include and how much to include. Materials were tested with classes of elementary education majors, music majors, and graduate students. The book evolved into a comprehensive overview of music for young children rather than a book of activities or a research monograph. Important components of this book including the references, charts, and resources are helpful for understanding the textual material such as books, songs, and assessment tools can be found on the author's Web site at <http://marvinmusic.org>. The resources include references, tables, and resources such as books, songs, and assessment tools.

I wish to acknowledge my children—Amanda, Christine, and Elisabeth—and the many children in classrooms who over the past thirty years shared their musical lives with me. I thank my professors at the University of Illinois who nurtured my interest in young children—R. Abramson, J. Frazee, M. Hoffman, L. Katz, C. Leonhard, R. B. Smith, and R. Thomas. I also wish to thank the creators of many methods discussed in Chapter 6 for their advice and review, and the many colleagues who reviewed either part or all of the text. Special thanks to the authors contributing chapters and sections—John Feierabend, Diane Persellin, Sandra Trehub, Joanne Rutkowski and Valerie Trollinger.

I am particularly indebted to Richard J. Colwell, editor, for guidance and for asking challenging questions. It is rare to find someone with such wide knowledge and experience in the field of music education that provides a *see the forest* editorial perspective that few texts, let alone series of texts, can boast.

1

Foundations:
The Context for Musical Lives
of Young Children

Introduction

Sound is among the earliest stimuli to have some form of meaning for the human being. Prenatal sound experiences influence the baby's preferences after birth. Researchers find that music helps premature infants gain weight and shortens their hospital stay (Standley, 2002). Within two months of birth, infants start phrasing vocalizations and begin to turn sounds into word play, an activity that continues long after the child can speak. Children develop in very individual ways and schedules. For example, one child may sing in tune at the age of two and another may not do so until five years of age. Research demonstrates that musicality is apparent in preverbal children, that infants are stimulated by musical games by the age of one, they enjoy playing with musical sounds, they display an inherent ability to move to music, and they can be better listeners than adults.

Babies can do much more than what was once thought. Gopnik, Meltzoff, and Kuhl write, "Babies and young children think, observe, and reason. They consider evidence, draw conclusions, do experiments, solve problems, and search for the truth." (1999, p. 13). While listening to music, for example, babies make fine musical discriminations of intervals, scales, and meter. Although babies often look very passive, research by Trehub and others (Chapter 4) indicates that a baby's listening is not so passive at it seems.

Young children from the prenatal experiences through young adulthood deserve the best possible music in their environment from their teachers and parents. Good models of singing, performing, and love of music will be mirrored in the young child's learning. Unfortunately, the young child also learns from bad musical models. For example, a child may engage in vocal activities that will physically damage vocal apparatus or movement activities that may cause injury (see Chapters 8–11 for details). Research on the human brain points to the importance of early experiences. Early care and nurture have a decisive, long-lasting impact on how people develop, their ability to learn, and their capacity to regulate their own emotions (Flohr, Miller, and Persellin, 2000). One of the twelve empirically based principles of child development and learning presented by the National Association for the Education of

1

Young Children (NAEYC) is that early experiences have both cumulative and delayed effects on individual children's development (Chapter 3). Optimal ages exist for certain types of development and learning.

Teachers of young children have long been viewed as being less knowledgeable and their work as less prestigious than that of an upper-level teacher. This specious logic extends to the length and quality of education that a teacher needs and therefore the belief that a college music teacher needs much more training than a teacher of young children. This logic is not only unfounded but dangerous. The logic stems from the opinion that children do not need to know much, anyone can teach them something worthwhile, and thus educational sophistication of the preschool teacher is not necessary. There is nothing farther from the truth. Young children deserve the best and most knowledgeable teachers as it is during the early years, prenatal to eight years of age, that the dispositions and groundwork for all future learning are laid (Katz and Chard, 1995). The present state of thought looks something like Figure 1.1, in which the emphasis of attention, resources, and prestige is on the upper levels of music education, but the foundations of music learning occur in early childhood and an inverted pyramid structure of emphasis leaves an inadequate foundation for many children. Several years ago, Brand (1985) noted how benefits to preschool children and their parents have traditionally been ignored by music educators. Informed opinion is changing and there is heightened interest in the benefits of early music education (Feierabend, 1995b; Flohr and Hodges, 2002; Gopnik et al., 1999; Levinowitz, 2001). States also are recognizing the value of early education and their funding for programs has increased from $190 million in 1988 to almost $2 billion in 2003 (Whitehouse, 2003). Twenty-six states target their programs to children from low-income families. Fifteen states and the District of Columbia have standards for prekindergarten with five more working on standards. In addition, an independent research and policy organization of business leaders and educators, the Committee for Economic Development (2002), underlines the value of preschool education with

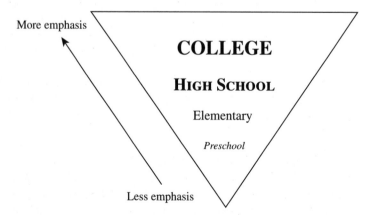

Figure 1.1 Emphasis of attention and resources in music education.

a call for access to high quality preschool classes for all children whose parents want them to participate.

Philosophy: How Does Music Function in People's Lives?

What function does music fulfill? Peery, Peery, and Draper examined several textbooks through 1982 and listed ten reasons writers cite for teaching music to young children (Peery, Peery, & Draper, 1987, p. 197). These reasons (in order of percentage of writers endorsing each reason) included: provides self-expression, fosters motor and rhythmic development, develops an aesthetic sense, teaches vocal and language development, promotes cultural heritage, promotes cognitive development, teaches social skills, promotes good self-esteem, provides release of tensions and aggression, and develops musicians.

A major U.S. national policy act gives the arts a firm position in the schools and additional reasons for teaching music to young children. Public Law 117-110, entitled *Elementary and Secondary Education Act* or *No Child Left Behind of 2001*, includes the arts in the definition of core academic subjects. Title IX, part A–definitions, Section 9101 (11) of the law defines core academic subjects, "The term core academic subjects means English, reading or language arts, mathematics, science, foreign languages, civics and government, economics, arts, history, and geography" (U.S. Department of Education, 2003).

The categories of extrinsic musical benefits and intrinsic musical benefits are helpful in discussions about the value of music in a child's education. Extrinsic benefits are those benefits that are outside of music. Extrinsic music benefits for young children include fosters motor development, promotes cultural heritage, provides release of tension, teaches language development, music as a carrier of information (e.g., *ABC* song), music as a cue for naptime, and using music to help teach other subjects such as reading or mathematics.

One philosophical concern with extrinsic benefits is that there are usually other ways of achieving these benefits. However, music has important worth in and of its self in addition to its use to achieve academic and personal purposes. Music clearly belongs in the young child's life as a distinct discipline and as an art form. What are often called intrinsic benefits of music education include self-expression (Peery et al., 1987), as well as emotional expression and aesthetic enjoyment (Elliott, 1997; Leonhard and House, 1972; Merriam, 1964; Reimer, 1970/1989, 2002). The intrinsic benefits are those benefits accomplished so well by music and for which other subjects are clearly less effective.

Music is a part of culture. Teachers need to be aware of the influence of the social context on the learning process in music. Marie McCarthy writes, "[M] usic education philosophers are increasingly coming to view music as social action and to consider music teaching and learning as a process that is embedded in social and cultural values and meanings" (2002, p. 563). Knowledge of the social and cultural contexts in which children live helps ensure that musical experiences are meaningful, relevant, and respectful for the children and their families. NAEYC standards support McCarthy's statement and remind us that learning occurs in and is influenced by multiple social and cultural contexts.

A Very Brief Look at the History of Music in Childhood

Music for young children began before the twenty-first century. Preschool music education began more than three hundred years ago with the general preschool movement. Education, child development, and play theories developed by Europeans including Comenius (1592–1670), Rousseau (1712–1778), Pestalozzi (1746–1827), and Froebel (1782–1852) helped forge present practice in early childhood education and early childhood music education (McDonald and Simons, 1989, pp. 4–19). Music was part of the general preschool movement. Music techniques applicable to young children have also been around for a long time. A thousand years ago in Italy Guido de Arezzo (born c. 995) became the first individual to be associated with what is currently called solfège, the use of syllables to designate the degrees of the musical scale. Solfège (also called solfa or solmization) technique has become a foundation for teaching music. The Hungarian composer Zoltán Kodály used a combination of solfège and hand signals to formulate his more structured method of teaching music (see Chapter 6). In the past one hundred years, teachers, composers, and entrepreneurs have developed additional methods and teaching techniques applicable to childhood and adults.

Twenty-First-Century Music for Young Children
Objectives of This Text

The primary objective of this text is to enable the prospective teacher, parent, or caregiver to understand, promote, and use music in young children's education. The focus is on what is known about music in childhood and how to apply this knowledge to the **craft** of teaching (Colwell and Wing, 2004). It is not about how to perform music for children or the role and importance of the teacher's personality, enthusiasm, or motivation. Study of this text will enable the reader will be able to understand issues and methodologies, identify milestones in children's development, and know how to organize and implement music experiences.

Unique Features of This Text

Several items in this text are unique and helpful in learning about music and young children: (1) Much of the research reviewed has never before been published in a summary text. (2) Summary tables of research, methods, and development are included for quick reference and to encourage discussion on how research may influence practice in the classroom and home. (3) What should happen with children and how a teacher or parent can make things happen are outlined in tables and experiences. (4) Practical suggestions and plans based on research for best practice including milestones of development in listening, singing, moving, creating, playing, reading, and writing. Benefits include practical information (e.g., what to do) and depth of scholarly research. (5) The author's Web site, <http://www.marvinmusic.com> contains more resources and a complete reference list..

Book Structure

This text is an overview and introduction to the field of music for young children and provides direction for teacher and parent. It is not a research compilation nor is it an activity-based book for teachers. Figure 1.2 illustrates the overall structure.

Part I, Foundations, outlines background information on child development, music in infancy, developmentally appropriate practices, and research findings about musical development. Included are overviews of education development theory that provide a picture of how children learn and develop, and a brief overview of methodologies.

Part II, Delivery: Methods and Organization, is divided into two major headings. First, ways of teaching children (methods) are described and compared. Second, organizing delivery is discussed with attention to method, national standards, objectives, lesson planning, and assessment.

Part III, Delivery: Experiences, is divided into chapters for each of the avenues of music learning; listening, singing, moving, creating, playing, reading, and writing (Leonhard and House, 1972). The examination of each avenue of music learning helps organize and apply research findings to teaching children. Part III contains summaries of studies and reviews of literature, developmental milestones, key points, pitfalls to avoid, examples of experiences, steps to successful experiences, as well as a chapter on integrating music with other subjects. Research to avenues of music learning enables teachers of young children and researchers to determine what

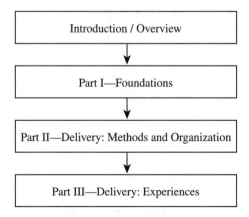

Figure 1.2 Schematic of book structure.

is best for children and what may be recommended as good practice. Visit the author's Web site for additional resources.

How to Use This Book

The task at hand is to apply interest, knowledge, and understanding of music—at whatever level that may be—to the music education of young children. The common definition of early childhood education includes children from birth to the elementary school age of eight years (NAEYC, 1997). For the purposes of this text, the emphasis is on children six years of age and younger, including prenatal music experiences. Information about teaching music to children of ages six to eight years is used in this text to highlight differences.

Figure 1.3 illustrates how to build the basis for musical experiences with children. Busy teachers or caregivers often think first about what to do with the children on Monday morning. A teacher, for example, thinks about the activities, the materials needed, and the time allocated for music. Concentrating on activities alone does not promote learning. Before choosing activities (the leaves of the tree), formulate a

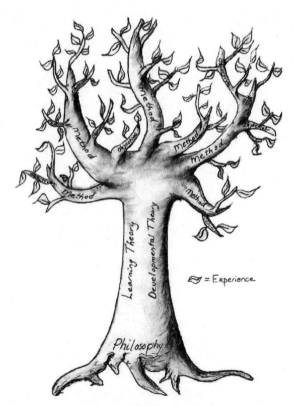

Figure 1.3   Foundations of music learning.
Illustrated by V. L. Trollinger

clear idea of what music means (philosophical foundation or philosophical root system), understand learning theories and their application to teaching, apply methods of teaching, and plan ways to connect objectives to the experiences offered to the children.

Use this text to gain an overview of music in childhood and to provide an outline for your **craft** of teaching young children.

2

Foundations: Theories and Approaches

Diane Cummings Persellin

To become an effective teacher of young children, it is important to understand how they learn. Such understanding provides a good foundation for the study of children and how they learn music. Learning theories help teachers plan strategies for teaching and set the environment as children develop skills, knowledge, and values. This chapter provides a brief overview of learning theories that are relevant to both young children's education and music education. Music applications of these theories are discussed in Chapter 3.

Learning Theories

Since the beginning of the twentieth century, a number of important thinkers and researchers have developed learning theories in order to better understand how children develop mentally and emotionally. Most of these theorists are well-known—at least by name; they are discussed in some detail elsewhere in this series. For the purpose of a quick review, Table 2.1 gives a brief summary of the most important and influential of these learning theories. We begin our review with Jerome Bruner who ushered in contemporary learning theories. Reinforcement and need theories are historically important with their salient ideas retained in the cognitive theories that range from direct instruction to constructivism.

Bruner's Modes of Representation

Jerome Bruner (1971) described three stages in which learners translate experiences into a model of the world: **enactive** (sensing, doing, and acting on the environment), **iconic** (imaging the experience through visual or other sensory icons that look like what the concept means), and **symbolic** (representing the experience through language or another system). For example, a child learning to read notation of a melody would first show the high and low pitches with her hand or body (enactive), then would read high and low line drawings or icons that represent the pitch (iconic), and finally would read the melody (notation) on a musical staff (symbolic).

Bruner was an advocate of the **discovery method** of learning. This method encourages children to explore and manipulate ideas. Children are challenged to

8

Table 2.1   Overview of Theories Relating to Young Children's Education

THEORY	THEORISTS	KEY PRINCIPLES AND MODELS	INSTRUCTIONAL STRATEGIES
8 psychosocial stages of human development	Erik Erickson	Humans must resolve key conflict during each of eight stages before proceeding to the next stage of development.	Teachers need knowledge of children's needs, interests, abilities and development.
Behaviorism	Skinner, Pavlov, & Watson	Positive/negative reinforcement, operant conditioning, successive approximation, transfer of knowledge.	Teachers use reinforcement (drilling, practicing, cueing) for correct response.
Social Learning	Albert Bandura	Children see models of behavior that can be replicated.	Modeling, reinforcement, personal evaluation
Piaget's Stage Dependent Theory	Jean Piaget	Four stages: sensorimotor (0-2), preoperational (2-7), concrete operations (7-11), & formal operations (11 to adult).	Teachers observe learners to determine stage of learning and to plan appropriate strategies.
Modes of Representation	Jerome Bruner	Children move through three stages of learning	Enactive: moving, and doing. Iconic: graphic images, line drawings. Symbolic: language, musical notation.
Maslow's Hierarchy	Abraham Maslow	Children are motivated by five basic stages of needs: physical, safety & security, belonging and affection, self-esteem, self-actualization.	Strategies include: observing to see that children are well-fed, safe and welcomed in the classroom; encouraging children to succeed.
Bloom's Taxonomy	Benjamin Bloom	Six levels of thought processes in a hierarchical taxonomy from simple to complex encourage teachers to use higher order thinking skills.	Teachers use all six with emphasis on more complex teaching strategies & asking questions.
Meaningful Reception	David Ausubel	Learning takes place when information is stored in organized ways.	Explanations, advanced organizers, demonstrations.
Multiple Intelligences	Howard Gardner	One learns through one or more of eight intelligences: linguistic, logical-mathematical, spatial, body-kinesthetic, musical, interpersonal, intrapersonal, naturalist.	Instructional strategies for each intelligence are created.
Learning Styles	Rita & Kenneth Dunn	Learning is affected by environmental, emotional, social, and physical factors.	Learners are more successful when teaching takes into account these factors.
Learning Modalities	Barbe and Swassing	Learners process information through preferred channels: auditory, visual, and/or kinesthetic.	Teachers teach through learning channels.
Constructivism	Vygotsky, Dewey, Piaget, DeVries, Kohlberg	Learners develop understanding of the world through their experiences.	Problem-solving, scaffolding, learning from environment, peer interaction.
Discovery Learning	Jerome Bruner	Learners develop a deep understanding of ideas by experimenting and forming their own concepts before it is labeled.	Children problem solve by exploring; guided to understanding and then given the label for the concept.
Ecological Psychology	Bronfenbrenner	Interactions with others and the environment are key to development.	Social environments (family, school community) stressed.

problem solve by taking risks, experimenting, and are then guided toward an understanding and the name of what they have been doing (see Chapter 6, Montessori). Bruner also stated that while some topics are best learned through the discovery method, others are not. A decision about when to use the discovery method and when to use a more direct or expository approach is a difficult decision and part of the craft or art of teaching. Much direct or expository instruction has behavioral or semi-behavioral objectives, goals, or aims.

Bloom's Taxonomy

Benjamin Bloom identified six levels of thought processes in a hierarchical taxonomy from simple to complex (Bloom and Krathwohl, 1956). These six levels encourage teachers to use higher order thinking skills in their questioning and in their creating teaching strategies; (1) *Knowledge.* Simple recall of facts or labeling. ("Who were the characters in the story about instruments that we heard yesterday?"); (2) *Comprehension.* Ability to manipulate, reconstruct, and summarize knowledge. ("Let's tell that story again from the beginning."); (3) *Application.* Ability to take information and apply it to another task. ("This time let's add instruments as we tell that story."); (4) *Analysis.* Ability to break knowledge into parts and show relationships among parts. ("What instruments should be played when the three bears walk upstairs?"); (5) *Synthesis.* Ability to take parts of a whole and reorder or create a new product. ("Lets create a song for the ending of our story using tone bells."); (6) *Evaluation.* Ability to assess the value of a product. ("What would you change about the way we told the story with instruments?")

Ideally, teachers are engaging children in all six levels with more emphasis on the complex levels (four-six). Classroom observations (Watkins, 1993) indicate, however, that 99 percent of questions asked by teachers are lower level questions. See Colwell and Wing (2004) for more information on Bloom.

Multiple Intelligences

A theory of multiple intelligences was developed and modified by Howard Gardner (1983; 1999a). This theory suggests that the traditional notion of intelligence, based on IQ testing, is far too limited. Instead, Gardner proposed seven, and later eight, intelligences to account for a broader range of human potential in children and adults (Gardner, 1993). It is interesting to note that his initial work on multiple intelligences was done with three- and four-year-olds. These intelligences are Verbal/Linguistic, Logical/Mathematical, Spatial, Body/Kinesthetic, Musical, Interpersonal, Intrapersonal, and Naturalist.

Learning Styles

Learning styles deal with how children prefer to learn and the environment that they choose when learning. Dunn and Dunn (1984) proposed that many factors affect learning. These factors include emotional, sociological, physical, and environmental influences such as sound, light, temperature, and food. For example, if children are uncomfortable or distracted, they may not be interested in singing or learning as effectively as they could.

Barbe and Swassing (1979) suggest that learning modality preferences are a specific type of learning style. They state that learners prefer to process information through one or a combination of several sensory channels: **auditory** (this child learns best by hearing and prefers verbal instructions and other aural input from the teacher or other students), **visual** (this child learns best by seeing and prefers to see a presentation and read instructions), and/or **kinesthetic** channels (this child learns best by moving, participating, touching, and being physically involved in the learning process). Effective teaching involves all three modalities. Teachers are encouraged to teach to a child's strongest modality and reinforce through the other two modalities. If faced with twenty children with various preferred modalities, it is best to use several modalities in all instruction (Persellin, 1993). The kinesthetic modality is especially appropriate for young children and music.

Constructivism

The constructivist theory states that children learn best when they are active learners and interact with the environment. The role of the educator is that of a facilitator setting up an environment conducive to learning (DeVries and Kohlberg, 1987; Vygotsky, 1962) (see Table 2.2).

John Dewey was among the first to seriously promote a constructivist approach. He advocated a child-centered curriculum in which active learning, music, and the other arts played an important role. Intellectual development was encouraged through problem solving, discovery, and exploration (Dewey, 1966).

Table 2.2   Selected Instructional Approaches for Young Children

APPROACH	DEVELOPER	SUMMARY
Constructivist	Dewey, Piaget, Vygotsky, DeVries, Kohlberg	Children are active learners and interact with environment to bring personal meaning to the topic. Teachers may scaffold or structure experiences.
High /Scope	David Weikart	Children participate in key experiences in cognitive, social, and physical development. Initial focus was providing quality program for low-income children.
Multiple Intelligences	Howard Gardner	Eight different intelligences account for a broader range of human potential in children and adults.
Montessori	Maria Montessori	Observation, individual liberty, and preparation of environment are stressed. Teachers work to control environment rather than children.
Project Approach	John Dewey	Children learn from participating in projects both in and out of classroom involving in-depth study.
Reggio Emilia Approach	Malaguzzi, parents, and teachers in Italy	Children learn from participating in projects and investigations with teachers as partners in learning. Children document their learning through art projects.
Waldorf Schools	Rudolph Steiner	Curriculum balances academic subjects with artistic, spiritual, and practical activities.

The basic principles of constructivist thinking can be summarized as follows: (1) Constructing meaning is learning. Learners construct knowledge for themselves; (2) Learning is an active process in which the learner uses sensory input and constructs meaning out of it; (3) Teachers provide learners with opportunities to interact with sensory data, and to construct their own world. Children's prior knowledge and interests should be used when planning instruction. The development of independence is a primary aim of education; (4) Vygotsky (1962) refers to the **zone of proximal development**. This is an area of development between a level in which the child has achieved competence and a higher level in which the child is not yet competent. The **zone** is the in-between area from which the child may reach out to an adult for help in understanding. The teacher can then plan activities within this **zone** in order to **scaffold** (Vygotsky's term) or provide structure to learning; (5) Vygotsky described the importance of language in learning and creating new thoughts and acquiring new knowledge; (6) Learning is a social activity. Conversation, interaction with others, and the application of knowledge are all integral aspects of learning. Discussion and problem solving between children and adults help children become socialized within their culture (Vygotsky, 1978); (7) Learning is contextual. We learn in relationship to what else we know, what we believe, our prejudices, and our fears; (8) The importance of play. Teachers need to provide children, especially young children, many opportunities to play. Musical play may include instrumental exploration, singing with puppets, ordering and classifying sounds, and improvising music. Through various types of play, a child's conceptual abilities are stretched.

Summary of Learning Theories

While learning theorists struggle to classify learning theories into discrete categories, one model has been proposed. Three broad categories—mechanistic, organismic, and contextual—may be used to examine the theories discussed in the previous section. Early theories may be categorized as mechanistic or organismic models (Overton, 1984). The mechanistic model views children as passive and their learning largely determined by environmental influences. The learning theories developed by Watson and Skinner favor the mechanistic view. The organismic model views children as active in learning and their development largely determined by influences within themselves. The theories of Piaget and constructivism fit the organismic model. The third broad category, contextual (Shaffer, 2002, p. 63), views children as active learners and development is determined by the interplay between environment (nurture) and children's individual characteristics (nature). The theories of Vygotsky and Bronfenbrenner come closest to the contextual model (see Table 2.1).

Approaches for Young Children

Montessori

The Montessori method was developed from the work of Italian physician, Dr. Maria Montessori (1870–1952). She observed that children who were free to participate in activities of their own choice appeared to become self-disciplined. They also were able to more fully focus their attention and interest on intellectual activity (Standing, 1957). The Montessori method is based on the human tendencies to explore, move, share with a group, be independent and make decisions, create order, develop self-control, form concepts from experiences, use the imagination, concentrate, and perfect one's efforts and creations (Lillard, 1996; Montessori, 1948, 1949, 1956; Morrison, 1998).

Principles of the Montessori method include (1) *Respect for the child.* Montessori stressed that children are not miniature adults. Children should be treated with respect and as unique individuals. Children should have freedom to be independent and make decisions. (2) *Prepared environments.* Teachers work to control the environment rather than control the children. They prepare and adapt the environment, link children to it through well-thought-out lessons, and facilitate the children's exploration and creativity. (3) *Absorbent mind self-education.* Montessori believed that human beings are not educated by another person; rather, they educate themselves. Young children educate themselves unconsciously and absorb knowledge simply by living. After the age of three, the absorbent mind is more selective and learning becomes more conscious. (4) *Sensitive periods.* Montessori believed there are sensitive periods of time when children can learn new specific skills more easily than at other times of development. In describing sensitive periods she wrote, "It is a transient disposition and limited to the acquisition of a particular trait. Once this trait or characteristic has been acquired, the special sensibility disappears" (Montessori, 1966, pp. 46, 49). For example, children will probably not learn nuances of language so they sound like a native speaker when the sensitive period for language is past (e.g., after age six or seven). (5) *Three stages of learning.* Children are first introduced to a concept through a lecture, lesson, or reading. They then begin to develop an understanding of the concept through independent exploration and creativity through interaction, problem solving, and socializing. An understanding of the lesson is then achieved and children are able to teach other children the concept.

Project Approach

The Project Approach is a set of teaching strategies in which children actively engage in in-depth studies of topics of interest. The goal of a project is to learn more about the topic rather than to seek right answers to questions posed by the teacher. Children are involved in discussions, dramatic play, construction, and creating charts and murals when working on a project. A project has three phases (Katz and Chard, 2000).

Phase 1: Beginning the project. The teacher discusses the topic with children to determine prior experiences and prior knowledge, then helps children develop questions that the project investigation may answer.

Phase 2: Developing the project. Opportunities for children to do fieldwork and speak to experts are arranged. The teacher and children gather help from resources such as real objects, books, and other research materials.

Phase 3: Concluding the project.   The teacher arranges a culminating event that gives children the opportunity to share their findings. The teacher then uses children's ideas and interests to make a meaningful transition between the project being concluded and the next topic of study.

Reggio Emilia

Reggio Emilia refers to a collection of twenty-two preschools in the small northern Italian city of Reggio Emilia. The groundwork for this approach was established shortly after World War II. Much of the Reggio Emilia approach to early education is aligned with Dewey, Piaget, Vygotsky, and Bruner and reflects a constructivist approach (Caldwell, 1997; Edwards et al., 1998; Katz and Cesarone, 1994; New, 1994, 2000). Reggio Emilia characteristics include:

1. The physical environment is crucial and emphasizes beautiful surroundings and openness. Displays of children's project work are interspersed with arrays of found objects and classroom materials throughout the school.
2. As children proceed in an investigation, they are encouraged to document their understanding through one of many symbolic modes of expression, including drawing, sculpture, dramatic play, shadow play, music, and writing, often referred to as the hundred languages of children. Visual art is a primary form and each classroom has a mini-atelier (small art studio).
3. Each center is staffed with two teachers per classroom, and an **atelierista** (a teacher trained in the arts) who works with classroom teachers.

High/Scope

The High/Scope Curriculum emphasizes active, child-initiated learning based on cognitive developmental and constructivist theory. The curriculum consists of fifty-eight well-defined key experiences in cognitive, social, and physical developmental areas that provide a framework for planning, guiding, and evaluating children's initiatives. The key experiences are grouped into ten categories: creative representation, language and literacy, initiative and social relations, movement, music, classification, seriation, number, space, and time (Hohmann and Weikart, 2002).

Learning centers contain books, blocks, computer, housekeeping, pretend, art, music, and sensory materials. These materials provide optimal opportunities for children's choices, for problem solving, social interaction, and independent thinking. The process of planning, doing, and then reviewing teaches children to make thoughtful choices, carry them out, and reflect on them.

The High/Scope Curriculum was developed in the 1960s and 1970s by the High/Scope Educational Foundation under the leadership of David Weikart (Schweinhart and Epstein, 1997; Weikart, 1996). Originally known as the Perry Preschool Project, was initially on effects of a high quality preschool program for low-income African-American children, the program has since expanded to encompass all types of early childhood centers. The results of a longitudinal research study have shown that participants in this program who were later interviewed at age twenty-seven have outperformed those without preschool in terms of educational attainment, income, and socially responsible behavior (Schweinhart and Weikart, 1997).

Waldorf Schools

The aim of Waldorf schooling is to educate the whole child, head, heart, and hands. Waldorf teachers are dedicated to creating a love of learning within each child. By freely using arts and activities in the service of teaching academics, an internal motivation to learn is developed in the students, doing away with the need for competitive testing and grading. Some distinctive features of Waldorf education include the following (Harwood, 1979; Steiner, 1982): (1) Academics are deemphasized in the early years of schooling. However, foreign languages are introduced at an early age. Children stay with the same lesson teacher for eight years; (2) Music, art, and gardening are stressed in the early years. All children learn to play recorder and to knit. Stringed instruments are introduced in third grade; (3) During the younger grades, all subjects are introduced through artistic mediums. It is believed that children respond better to this medium than to lecturing and rote learning; (4) Upper grades use textbooks to supplement their main lesson work. The use of television and computers by young children is strongly discouraged in Waldorf schools.

Summary

There are multiple paths to educate young children. Although the selected theories and approaches in this chapter reflect a wide range of thinking on the teaching and learning of young children, they do, however, share similarities. Most theories and approaches advocate active rather than passive learning, careful observing of children, and making learning meaningful to them. The fact that these theories and approaches still each have a following is a testimony to their effectiveness in the appropriate settings.

3
Foundations:
Music Learning and Development

Introduction

Childhood development and music development in childhood are complex topics. The more a teacher or parent understands how children develop musically, the better they are able to make decisions about what musical experiences to offer children and when to offer the experiences (Katz and Chard, 1995).

Issues

There are three major issues about how children learn and develop that may help us discuss theories of music learning and development. The first is the long-standing **nature versus nurture** issue and it is now accepted that both are important.

A second issue concerns the child as an **active versus passive** contributor to his/her own development. The third issue, **discontinuous versus continuous,** is concerned with whether the developmental changes occur in a discontinuous manner by stages or in a continuous manner. A key difference is whether the changes are quantitative, and with a sudden change, or a gradual differentiation from the previous stage. In music, for example, discontinuous learning would be represented if a seven-year-old child reached an "AHA" point and could now identify two selections of music as being similar that were the same in melody but different in terms of tempo, timbre, or rhythm (conservation). A child's gradual, incremental, and quantitatively higher scores on listening tests would represent continuous learning.

Before reading further, be sure to do the following exercises. What do you think about the three issues? Place yourself on the lines below. For example, if you think nature affects musical development more than nurture, make a mark to the left of the mid-point (for more on nature/nuture, see Pinker, 2002).

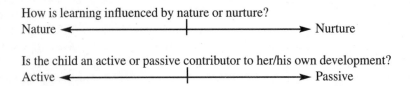

How is learning influenced by nature or nurture?
Nature ◄─────────────────┼─────────────────► Nurture

Is the child an active or passive contributor to her/his own development?
Active ◄─────────────────┼─────────────────► Passive

Is development continuous (gradual) or discontinuous (in stages, plateaus, sudden spurts, during sensitive periods, or limited windows of opportunity)?

Continuous ◄─────────────────┼──────────────────► Discontinuous

General Music Development

This section examines broad ideas and theories specific to music development. The NAEYC position statement document comments on general development include: "Because development and learning are so complex, no one theory is sufficient to explain these phenomena" (NAEYC, 1997). Unfortunately there is neither one readily accepted theory nor meta-theory in musical development. A complete discussion of musical development is beyond the scope of this text, but review resources are available on the author's Web site. In addition, the music experience chapters (listening, singing, creating, moving, playing, reading, and writing) each include a developmental milestone table. Table 3.1 provides a brief overview of research studies described by the two issues of **active versus passive** and **discontinuous versus continuous,** and summary categories from Chapter 2 (**mechanistic, organismic, contextual**).

Table 3.1 illustrates that all but the earliest of the selected musical development studies and theories favor the active learner concept and several are based on Piaget's stage theory. The dimension of **continuous versus discontinuous** is more complex and varied, but there is a trend toward the discontinuous viewpoint. Research supports the stage theory of Piaget and the organismic model, but leans toward cumulative **layers** or **levels** rather than stages. The recent studies shown in Table 3.1 and developmental theory (e.g., Vygotsky and Bronfenbrenner) support continuity in development and the contextual model.

Overview of Music Development Theory

Over two thousand years ago, Plato described the use of music with infants (West, 2000). The Chinese people have a long history of stressing importance of prenatal education and call it **Tai-Jiao** (Fetus-Education). In the 1930s, researchers began to document prenatal response to sounds from the environment (Sontag and Wallace, 1935). Later documentation has included how the child might hear within the womb, how the prenatal child learns from interaction with the environment, neonatal responses (immediately after birth), and postnatal results of prenatal stimulation (Lecanuet, 1996; Standley and Madsen, 1990, pp. 60–67 for a review; Trevarthen, 1999–2000). Table 3.2 illustrates the child's development in terms of music and hearing from embryo to the end of the first year of life.

The environment of the womb is not a quiet environment. *The Secret Life on the Unborn Child* brought attention in the early 1980s to the possibilities of growth and development in utero (Verny, 1981). During the third trimester of life fetuses: (1) have functional auditory systems, (2) are able to hear and are responsive to externally produced sound as well as maternal sounds, and (3) react to sudden changes in auditory stimulation. Neonatal and post birth studies demonstrate evidence for memory

Table 3.1   Selected Music Development Research

STUDY OR THEORY	ACTIVE PASSIVE	CONTINUOUS DISCONTINUOUS	MODEL	SUMMARY
Pflederer (1964)	Active: Piaget	Stage: emphasis on stages such as conservation	Organismic	Landmark pilot study applying Piaget's theory to music development. From 1964 several studies examine conservation and other Piagetian tasks (Zimmerman & Sechrest, 1968; Zimmerman, 1982).
Petzold (1966)		Discontinuous: plateau	Organismic	Age is a major factor in development of auditory perception. A plateau at age 8. Much development between 6 and 7 years (2 years to show much progress).
Symbol system approach—Gardner (1973); Davidson (1994)	Active	Phases	Organismic	Development related to the acquisition & use of symbols. Significant changes between the ages of 5 and 7 years. Also evidence of developmental phases in understanding of tonal contour (see also Davidson & Scripp, 1988; Davidson & Colley, 1987).
Moog (1976)				A large study of music development of children 6 months to 5½ years. See also ch. 10, Moving.
Rider (1981)	Active: Piaget	Stage	Organismic	Example of music therapy performance based developmental study common in special education fields. Piaget visual tasks were used to devise 15 auditory tasks. Rider summarizes the number of children passing a task such as loudness discrimination and the age/grade at which 50% or more children pass each task.
Regelski (1982)	Active, constructivist			Believes children should be more actively involved in music making rather than emphasizing verbal knowledge.
Sloboda (1985)	Active; reflective awareness	Continuous; linear progression	Contextual	Much of music cognitive development occurs between 5-10 years of age.
Categorizing—Cutietta (1985)				The mind categorizes musical sounds in a holistic way (in contrast to the elements of music fashion such as pitch, rhythm, timbre). First grade children make fine discriminations for categories of music (Lineburgh, 1994). 3 to 5-year-olds with training are able to predict chord changes (Berke, 2000). See also Cutietta & Haggerty (1987); Zwink (1988).
Swanick & Tilman (1986)	Active	Discontinuous: age related trends	Organismic	Several broad age levels of development (0-4; 4-9; 10-15; 15+). Spiral development similar to MMCP (Biasini, 1970).
Dowling (1988)	Active	Continuous	Contextual	Cultural dependent pattern and tonal **invariants** develop from birth to 8.

Note: All column categories are not meant to be complete for all studies or theories.

Table 3.1 Continued

STUDY OR THEORY	ACTIVE PASSIVE	CONTINUOUS DISCONTINUOUS	MODEL	SUMMARY
Music as cognition Serafine (1988)	Active & constructive process	Discontinuous: Piaget based	Organismic	Style specific & generic processes present in cognition of music (the development of thought in sound) grouped into temporal and nontemporal. Rapid growth in cognition between 8-10 years.
Boardman (1988; 1989)	Active: child is free to construct learning	Discontinuous: enumerates stages of melodic & rhythmic development.	Contextual	Generative approach to music learning—purpose of learning is to generate more learning. Based on early writings of Bruner (Ch. 2). See also Bergethon, Boardman & Montgomery (1996). Contextual in sense that the environment should encourage exploration & problem solving.
Sims (1988, 1991)	Active	Indication of Piaget age differences.	Organismic	Movement behaviors indicated age-related differences (4-9 years) on discrimination tasks that could partly be explained by Piagetian theory. With training the 4-5 year olds performed better on single discriminations but not for double discriminations. Piaget noted a centration quality, ability to center on only one perceptual characteristic at a time, in children younger than seven years.
Bamberger (1991, 1994, 2000)	Active	Continuous: levels rather than stages.	Contextual	Figural and formal hearing (see Ch. 11). She studied musical behavior as it occurs in a social context.
Gordon (1994, 1997)	Active	Both. Sequential development in tonal & rhythm patterns.	Organismic	Central concept–audiation–is the ability to hear and comprehend in the mind, the sound of music that is no longer or may never have been present (1976). Three types and 7 stages of preparatory audiation + 8 types and 6 stages of audiation. Audiation ideally begins about 5 years of age. Gordon developed a parallel between language and musical development. Developmental music aptitude—by age 9 where aptitude for music stabilizes.
5-7 year shift (1995, 1996)	Active	Continuous with discontinuous shift.	Organismic	Development is continuous but a significant change occurs between 5 & 7 years. See Davidson and Flohr & Miller (1995); Janowsky & Carper (1996).
Hargreaves & North (2000-1)	Active	Continuous; age a factor.	Organismic	The effect of a MIDI condition (the children heard live performance of the transformations) may indicate that prior music conservation tasks are flawed because during those tasks the children were unable to observe the transformation of the stimuli. Points toward continuous development although the older children outperformed the young children.
Holgersen (2002)	Active	Continuous; A child's strategies are non-hierarchical, varied and do not occur in a linear progression but at random	Contextual is closest match	Based on the theory of Merleau-Ponty–**lived body**–that each child is an integrated unit in which our senses, emotions, knowledge, and gender function together. The child is being directed toward and by something meaningful. **Participant strategies** (Holgersen, 2002) and **musical attunement** (Fink-Jensen, 1997) promote understanding of the meaning that music activities offer children in varying situations.

Table 3.2 Overview of Prenatal-First Year Musical Development

TRIMESTER	PERIOD	WEEK	MAJOR DEVELOPMENTS
First	Embryo	3–4	The embryo is only ¼" in size but the brain, spinal cord, and heart are forming.
		4–9	The ear is forming and particularly susceptible to harm from harmful agents such as disease, drugs, or any environmental agent. Continued susceptibility to full term.
Second	Fetus	9–12	Rapid growth. Organs become interconnected.
	Fetus	13–24	DeCasper & Fifer (1980) summarize that prenatal auditory experience is sufficient to influence postnatal auditory preferences. For example, neonates prefer their mother's voice to the voices of other women (see also DeCasper & Spence, 1986). Lecanuet (1996) review on prenatal auditory experiences.
		18	Bones of inner ear and neural connections to brain develop. Child hears sounds such as heartbeat. Loud sounds may cause heart rate to increase.
		20	Bones of middle ear and cochlea begin to harden.
	Premature birth	22–28	Age of viability. Lorch et al. (1994) found calming and sedative effects of 2 styles of music; impact of sedative & stimulating music was sometimes reversed from what one might expect (e.g., heart rate lower for stimulating music). If born premature will have a chance to survive. Standley (1998; 2002) summarizes many benefits of music for premature infants including calming, weight gain, reducing stress behaviors, decreasing hospital stay, and increasing oxygen saturation levels. Found gender difference in relation to music effect—female infants were discharged earlier. Standley (2002) reports a meta-analysis of 10 studies showing a general positive and significant impact of music in ICU.
Third	Fetus	25–38	Loud conversations can be heard distinctly in the womb although the mother's abdominal wall reduces sound levels (approx. 15 decibels & especially sounds greater than 100 Hz). The mother's digestive system often reaches 75-85 decibels (Walker, Grimwade, & Wood, 1971; Birnholz, 1983). Nearby external speech & maternal speech can be heard over background noise; especially sounds over 100 Hz (Lecanuet, 1996). Fetus will show startle response to loud noises and ultrasound. They may respond to sound by moving or kicking (Campbell, 1985). Pregnant women notice a fetal jerk or kick after a sudden loud noise such as a car backfiring or slamming of a door. Hepper (1988) reported that a fetus will retain some memory of a frequently repeated auditory event. The media called the retention a fetal **soap addiction** (the music was from a soap opera) of the seven pregnant women's babies. Overall, the supportable notion is that a fetus will retain some memory of a frequently repeated auditory event. Woodward (1998) prepared a compact disc of recorded in utero to demonstrate how the child hears singing and other sounds.
		30–35	Fetus hears maternal and environmental sounds. Brain response to sound matures.

Table 3.2   Continued

TRIMESTER	PERIOD	WEEK	MAJOR DEVELOPMENTS
Birth	Neonate	1st week	Responds to bell, rattle, & voice during first 3 weeks (Bayley, 1969; Brazelton, 1973). Prenatal and postnatal exposure to a sound stimulus is more effective at soothing than the exposure is postnatal only or when there is no exposure to a specific lullaby (Polverini-Rey, 1992). Verny (1981) reports anecdotal accounts of adult memories of prenatal auditory stimulation (e.g., the son of a cellist who later became a conductor). Habituation studies indicate neonates are able to discriminate sounds that differ in loudness, duration, direction, and frequency (Bower, 1982). Woodward (1992) found evidence of memory/recognition of in utero music. Neonate can discriminate loudness and pitch (Hofer, 1981). Neonates differentiate music from noise and prefer music (Butterfield & Siperstein, 1972). Flohr, et al. (2000) found neonates using sucking device showed preference for style of music.
First year		Week	
		0–16	10-40% of infants are diagnosed with colic. Birns et al. (1965) found a low frequency tone inhibited crying more effectively than high frequency (high frequencies reduce crying to a lesser degree). Also, infants are less sensitive to low frequencies than to high frequencies (Trehub, Schneider, & Endman, 1980). Common factor in infant soothing is rhythmic stimulation perhaps because rhythmic stimulation mirrors biological rhythms (Lester & Boukydis, 1985). Infants prefer motherese over adult directed speech (Fernald, 1989), infant-directed singing over adult directed singing (Trainor, 1996), are sensitive to music phrase structure (Krumhansl & Jusczyk, 1990), are sensitive to rhythm patterning, simple melody & harmony, timbre & melodic contour (Schellenberg & Trehub, 1996; Thorpe & Trehub, 1989; Trehub, 1990; Trehub, Bull, & Thorpe, 1984). See Chapter 4 for a discussion of music in infancy. Non-contingent music selected by parent had no effect on colic but contingent music with parent attention led to substantial decrease (Larson & Ayllon, 1990).
		0–52	Illari (2002a) found mothers who spend large amounts of time with their infants are not taking advantage of the benefits of musical activities as they might. For a review see Ilari (2002b). Vocalizes in response to attention; imitates adult, claps hands (pat-a-cake); imitates adult, squeezes or shakes toy to produce sound; imitates movement of another child (Doan, Wollenburg, & Wilson, 1994). Babbling begins to resemble language and many children produce their first words.
		12–20	Transfers musical instrument from hand to hand (Michel & Rohrbacher, 1982).
		16–24	Turns to sound source; responds to music with repetitive movements; musical babbling (Moog, 1976b).
		24–52	Shakes bell or other small instrument; uses at least 3 different hand movements to music/rhythmic response (Michel & Rohrbacher, 1982). Cheour et al. (1998) find native and foreign language stimuli (Finnish & Estonian) produced different left hemisphere brain activity at 12 months than at 6 months. Language dependent memory traces in the brain emerge before 12 months. Primary emotions appear; child can discriminate facial expressions such as happiness, anger, and sadness.
	1	36–44	Pokes piano key with isolated index finger (Michel & Rohrbacher, 1982).
	1	40	Infant startled at 90-decibel sound (DiCarlo & Bradley, 1961).

and recognition of music heard in utero. In addition to Sandra Trehub's review and poignant glimpse of music in infancy (Chapter 4), studies with infants through one year of age show prenatal and postnatal soothing effects of music for crying and colic, infant preferences for music and voices, and evidence that infants are sensitive to many qualities of music (Table 3.2) (H. Papoušek, 1996).

Because infants cannot talk and explain what they see and hear, researchers use four methods to make sense out of infants' sensory and perceptual experiences (Shaffer, 2002, p. 182). In the preference method researchers offer the infant at least two stimuli and observe what stimuli the infant attends to the most (Fantz, 1963). Habituation, the process whereby a repeated stimulus becomes familiar so that responses no longer occur, is a very popular method (e.g., head turn—see Chapter 4, heart rate changes). Measuring the electrical current of the brain on the scalp gives information (Cheour et al., 1998; Flohr and Hodges, 2002). Electrodes placed on the scalp measure the small electrical impulses with techniques called EEG (electroencephalography) and ERP (event-related potentials derived from EEG). The fourth way is with a nonnutritive sucking device. The special pacifier contains pressure sensitive devices connected to an electrical signal that enables the infant to control selection of stimuli based on the way which she/he sucks on the pacifier (Standley, 1999).

Many CDs and tapes are designed for pregnant women and their babies. Quality instrumental music for prenatal and infant listening is often recommended (Flohr, 2001). Trehub (1990) identifies suitable infant music to be music similar to what infants usually hear under natural circumstances, that is, voices of children or young females in infant-directed nursery songs. Good examples of quality vocal and instrumental music are available for infants, young children, and children in utero (prenatal) (Feierabend, 2000b; Flohr, 2001; Lloyd, Pratt, Coleman, and Colemnan, 1999; Thurman and Langess, 1986; Zemke, 1989). While many styles of music are probably good for children, music for pregnant women and their babies should be carefully chosen. Lecanuet (1996) offers an excellent review of the issues involved in using headphones, speakers, and other auditory stimulation during the prenatal period. The way in which the sound is administered—airborne sound, air-coupled sound, and vibratory sound (touching the mother's abdomen)—affects the quality of the sound transferred to the infant. Loud stimuli (over one hundred decibels) induce heart rate acceleration usually accompanied by a motor response.

A child's musical ability is important information to obtain because it helps parents and teacher make better decisions about experiences, objectives, and curriculum (see Chapters 6–7). Colwell suggests that it may be best to think about music aptitude, talent, ability, musicality, and related terms as comparable (Colwell, 2002b). Runfola and Swanwick (2002) note that beginning with inherited musical talent in the 1930s there was a shift to use of the term musical intelligence, then music abilities, and finally music aptitude. For the purposes of this text music aptitude or talent is defined as the child's potential for learning music. Musical ability is defined as "what a person is *able* to do musically" (Boyle, 1992, p. 248).

The work of the educational psychologist Carol Dweck helps place the controversy regarding definitions of musical ability in perspective (Dweck, 1999). For example, she found that beliefs about intelligence being fixed or able to be developed are more or less equally divided among the individuals in her studies. If a child forms the belief that her music ability is fixed, the teacher and parent need to be aware of these beliefs and work toward convincing her that she can learn music skills and competencies. They also need to be aware that indiscriminate approval of music performance and skills may harm young children who have developed performance beliefs about musical competence. For example, if a teacher of a first grade class listens to the class sing a song and then tells them all, "Great job," when only one or two children are singing well, her positive reinforcement will be counterproductive. Such reinforcement may, to a degree, help those children believing in fixed talent, but harm those believing in developing talent by rewarding poor singing.

A music learning theorist and author of music tests, Edwin Gordon, suggests that music aptitude can be enhanced during early childhood (Gordon, 1997). His concept of developmental music aptitude is that it stabilizes around the age of eight or nine after which scores of children on music aptitude tests do not change to an appreciable degree. The extent to which one agrees with the idea of music aptitude as inherited (nature) or music aptitude as developing (nurture) will affect the way she or he teaches and encourages children. For example, if a parent thinks the environment has an effect, he or she will give the child early experiences in music.

Summary and Key Points

This chapter noted the complexity of learning and development. Because young children's development is so complex, it is best viewed from several perspectives including music, psychology and brain research, anatomy, and social setting. The nature versus nurture issue is largely resolved. Development is affected by multiple causes from nature and from nurture. Neither nature nor nurture alone determines brain development. There are both stages and continuity in development. Studies of musical development point toward cumulative layers rather than stages. Developmental sequences are recursive so that a teacher can review objectives such as maintain a steady beat at a deeper level each year or month. For example, in first grade, children tap or chant a steady beat to a moderate tempo; a deeper level of the task is to individually move to a steady beat. Children are active in their own development. Ideas such as *tabulae rasae* (blank slates) have been replaced by organismic and contextual views of development. When using prenatal auditory stimulation be careful with the loudness of music especially when instruments or speakers are touching the mother's abdomen. The unborn child is accustomed to hearing sounds from eighty to ninety-five decibels and will habituate to loud sounds (Lecanuet, 1996), but sudden peaks in volume especially over one hundred decibels result in a startle response with the infant kicking or waving their arms and legs.

4

Foundations:
Music Perception in Infancy

Sandra E. Trehub

This chapter takes a closer look at the first year of life and provides information about how children perceive music. Refer to Table 3.2 for an overview of music development from prenatal to one year of age.

Why Study Music in Infancy?

Most scientists, music educators, and laypersons believe that the ability to perceive and enjoy music arises largely from musical training or incidental exposure to music. It is possible, however, that nature endows human beings with rudimentary listening skills as well as rudimentary responses to music. One way of gaining insight into the initial musical state is to examine the musical skills and responsiveness of infants before their musical culture-to-be has had a chance to leave its indelible impression.

Music Listening Skills in Infancy

Test Procedures

How do researchers arrive at their conclusions about infants and music? Perhaps the greatest challenge of researchers in this field is finding a suitable means of evaluating the listening skills of preverbal infants. One prominent technique, **conditioned head turning,** involves the repeated presentation of a melody or tone sequence from a loudspeaker located to one side of the infant (Trehub, Bull, and Thorpe, 1984; Trehub, Thorpe, and Morrongiello, 1987). From time to time, the repeating pattern is replaced with a slightly altered pattern—one involving a change in pitch or timing. If infants turn to the loudspeaker immediately following the change, they are rewarded by a three-second view of a colorful animated toy. Turns at other times have no consequence. Infants six months of age or older learn this game readily, and they will usually play it for ten or fifteen minutes. If infants respond (i.e., turn) more frequently following changes in the melody than at other times, that indicates that they can detect the change. Infants' detection of changes also provides insight into their memory for various aspects of the original pattern. For example, infants' detection of

24

changes in the pitch or temporal patterning of a melody indicates that they noticed and remembered the original pitch or temporal patterning.

The head-turn preference procedure involves the presentation of contrasting musical patterns from two different loudspeakers (Trainor and Heinmiller, 1998). Infants' attention is attracted to one loudspeaker, at which time they hear one of two musical patterns. When infants look away from the loudspeaker, the music stops. On the next trial, infants' attention is attracted to the other loudspeaker, which presents the contrasting musical pattern. As before, the music stops when infants look away. After infants complete a series of such trials, their looking times toward each loudspeaker (i.e., for each musical sample) are tabulated. Longer looking to one loudspeaker than to the other, which corresponds to greater listening time, provides evidence that infants noticed the difference between the two patterns. It also indicates which of the two patterns infants prefer.

Relational Processing

Research with these procedures has revealed surprisingly good listening skills on the part of infants. After hearing a melody a few times, infants remember its overall pitch contour (Trehub et al., 1984) and rhythm (Chang and Trehub, 1977a; Trehub and Thorpe, 1989). Like adults, they can recognize a previously heard melody when they hear it in a different key (Chang and Trehub, 1977b; Trehub et al., 1987) or tempo (Trehub and Thorpe, 1989).

Consonant and Dissonant Intervals

In some circumstances, but not others, infants are able to detect interval changes. The circumstances that generate success or failure are especially intriguing. Infants detect interval changes in melodies that conform to the rules of Western musical structure, and they fail to detect interval changes in melodies that violate such rules. For example, they succeed with melodies based on the major triad but not with those based on the augmented triad or those involving dissonant melodic intervals (Cohen, Thorpe, and Trehub, 1987; Trainor and Trehub, 1993; Trehub, Thorpe, and Trainor, 1990). Some melodic and harmonic intervals, notably the perfect fifth and perfect fourth (frequency ratios of 3:2 and 2:1, respectively), are special for infants, as they are for adults, in contrast to the dissonant tritone (frequency ratio of 45:32), which poses difficulty for infants and adults (Schellenberg and Trehub, 1996a).

Infants also prefer consonant music to dissonant music. For example, they respond more positively to music from the traditional folk or "classical" repertoire than to "doctored" versions in which dissonant intervals replace some of the consonant intervals (Trehub and Heinmiller, 1998; Zentner and Kagan, 1996). These findings are consistent with the view that preferences for musical consonance are part of our biological heritage (Blacking, 1992). Similar factors may account for the prominence of consonant intervals across musical cultures (Sachs, 1943; Trehub, Schellenberg, and Hill, 1997).

Scales

Although scales differ from one culture to another, the feature of unequal scale steps is ubiquitous (Sloboda, 1985). For example, the Western major scale has two-semi-tone steps (e.g., *do–re*) and one-semitone steps (e.g., *ti–do*). In one study (Trehub, Schellenberg, and Kamenetsky, 1999), infants were required to detect a mistuned tone (three-quarter-semitone change) in ascending-descending scales of various types. Interestingly, they succeeded in the context of the major scale and an invented, unequal-step scale, but they failed when the mistuned tone occurred in an invented scale with equal steps (i.e., division of the octave into seven equal steps). This finding implies that unequal steps in scales facilitate perceptual processing and the retention of melodic information, just as consonant intervals do.

Meter

Adult-infant parallels are not limited to pitch processing. Infants remember more detail about musical patterns when the patterns are metric rather than nonmetric and when the patterns are in duple rather than triple meter (Bergeson, 2002). Infants are also more attentive to intact musical phrases from Mozart minuets than to compara-ble phrases that are disrupted by brief silent intervals (Krumhansl and Jusczyk, 1990).

Adult-Infant Differences

There are instances in which inexperienced infants outperform their musically experi-enced counterparts. As noted, infants more readily detect tuning changes in the context of scales with unequal steps than in those with equal steps (Trehub et al., 1999). Adults tested with similar materials show a different pattern of findings. Like infants, they per-form better on the major scale than on the artificial, equal-step scale. Unlike infants, however, they perform equally poorly on both artificial scales, regardless of the pres-ence of equal or unequal scale steps (Trehub et al., 1999). In other words, adults' per-formance in this situation is driven by familiarity rather than scale structure. Infants also outperform adults in detecting changes that are consistent with the implied har-mony of a melody (Trainor and Trehub, 1992). Because such changes do not alter the musical meaning, they tend to escape the attention of experienced listeners.

Caregivers' Music for Infants

Nature provides the perceptual foundations for music and its appreciation, but the process of musical enculturation begins at a relatively early age. In this regard, moth-ers serve as the principal mentors. Mothers talk to their infants using a style of speech that is imbued with musical qualities like rhythmicity, repetition, and simple pitch contours (Fernald, 1991; M. Papoušek, 1992). This musical speech style has been observed in mother-infant interactions across numerous cultures. Moreover, musical qualities like those in maternal speech are also evident in the speech that fathers (Fernald, 1989) and young children (Ninio and Snow, 1999) address to infants.

The musical qualities of speech to infants arise primarily from the emotional expressiveness of such speech. For example, adult-directed messages that express love or comfort are acoustically similar to those in infant-directed messages with comparable expressive intent (Trainor, Austin, and Desjardins, 2000). Similarly, adult-directed messages of surprise have acoustic parallels to infant-directed messages of surprise (Trainor et al., 2000). The implication is that caregivers' typical speech to infants is emotionally charged, unlike typical adult speech which is neutral in emotional tone. The emotion in mothers' speech to infants is likely to originate in positive feelings for the infant amplified by positive feedback from the infant.

Universal Pitch Contours and Unique Tunes

Fine-grained analyses of maternal speech to preverbal infants reveal that each mother uses a small set of tunes (i.e., interval sequences) that she fills with different verbal content at different times (Bergeson, 2002). Moreover, the tunes of each mother differ from those of every other mother.

Although the rhythmicity, repetitiveness, interval consistency, and simple pitch contours add a musical flavor to maternal speech, this speech is not musical in the strict sense nor do the intervals in these so-called tunes correspond to conventional intervals in Western music or in any other musical system. In principle, the consistency and individual distinctiveness of maternal tunes should facilitate infants' identification of the mother from her voice alone.

Maternal Singing

Mothers' vocal interactions with infants are not limited to speech. Mothers across cultures sing regularly to their infants (Trehub and Trainor, 1998; Tucker, 1984). Like maternal speech, maternal songs are rhythmic, repetitive, and melodically simple (Trehub, Unyk, and Trainor, 1993b; Unyk, Trehub, Trainor, and Schellenberg, 1992).

Aside from a distinctive song repertoire for infants, a distinctive performing style is also evident across cultures (Trehub et al., 1993a). The unique features of sung performances for infants include higher pitch level, slower tempo, and greater emotionality relative to typical informal singing (Trainor, Clark, Huntley, and Adams, 1997; Trehub, Unyk et al., 1997). Mothers' performances for infants are highly stereotyped in the sense that they typically sing specific songs at the same pitch level and tempo on different occasions (Bergeson and Trehub, 2002). The maternal style of singing is highly successful in maintaining infants' interest and regulating their arousal level (Masataka, 1999; Trainor, 1996; Trehub and Nakata, 2002).

Paternal and Fraternal Singing

Although fathers sing much less than mothers do, their performances are as emotive as those of mothers despite some differences in song selection and singing style (O'Neill, Trainor, and Trehub, 2001; Trehub, Hill, and Kamenetsky, 1997; Trehub, Unyk et al., 1997). Fathers typically generate more sex-typed performances than mothers do, for example, singing in a more soothing manner for their infant daughters and in a livelier manner for their infant sons (Trehub, Hill, and Kamenetsky 1997). Preschool children also alter their performances in the presence of their infant siblings, mainly by singing more exuberantly than otherwise (Trehub, Unyk, and Henderson, 1994).

Infants' Preference for Maternal Speech and Singing

There is considerable evidence that infants are more attentive to infant-directed speech than to adult-directed speech in the newborn period (Cooper and Aslin, 1990) and in the months that follow (Fernald, 1985). Infants seem to prefer speech with positive emotional tone (i.e., happy talk) to speech with neutral emotional tone, regardless of whether the speech is addressed to an infant or adult audience (Singh, Morgan, and Best, 2002).

When infants watch and listen to audiovisual versions of singing and speech featuring their own mother, they show considerably greater interest in the singing episodes than in the speech episodes (Nakata and Trehub, 2000). Not only do they look at the mother's on-screen image for much longer periods during the sung performance, but they decrease their body movements, as they do in situations of intense interest. In short, they give every indication of being mesmerized by their mother's singing. They remain captivated by such audiovisual performances of singing, even when the singer is someone else's mother rather than their own (Nakata and Trehub, 2001).

In addition to visible consequences of maternal singing, such as increased visual attention and decreased body movement, there are invisible but equally dramatic physiological consequences. In one study (Trehub, Nakata, and Shenfield, in preparation), mothers sang to their infants for ten minutes on one day and spoke to infants in comparable circumstances on another day. Infant saliva samples taken before and after singing were analyzed to yield cortisol levels, which provide a reliable index of stress or arousal. Maternal singing led to more sustained reductions in infant arousal than did maternal speech. Maternal singing seems to be much more effective than maternal speech in regulating the arousal of infants (Fernald, 1991). The success of maternal singing in regulating the arousal of preverbal infants may account for the ubiquity of singing to infants across cultures and historical periods (Trehub and Trainor, 1998). Maternal singing is also effective in reducing the arousal levels of very-low-birth-weight infants whose stress levels can be life-threatening (Standley and Moore, 1995). Interestingly, music continues to function as a regulator of arousal or mood well into adolescence and adulthood (Sloboda and O'Neill, 2001).

Summary and Music Education for Infants and Parents

Infants' exceptional music listening skills and their intense interest in music may make them seem like ideal music students—better, perhaps, than older children whose increased sophistication is often accompanied by skepticism about adult guidance. Moreover, contemporary parents have unparalleled enthusiasm for music, sometimes for the wrong reasons. In recent years, many parents have succumbed to intemperate claims in the media about music and intelligence. It all began with a report that ten minutes of listening to a Mozart sonata could enhance spatial reasoning skills and, by extension, intelligence (Rauscher, Shaw, and Ky, 1993). However, the much-touted **Mozart effect** turned out to be overrated. In short, music does not provide a magical route to general intellectual accomplishment. (As most of us know, hard work and intelligent parents function better in that regard.)

Non-"goal-oriented" parent-tot programs are more open-ended, both in philosophy and content. Instructors in these programs affirm the musical nature of participants by providing a relaxed atmosphere in which parents and infants can enjoy musical activities of various kinds. In such settings, some parents may reconnect with their distant musical past (e.g., childhood music lessons, the joy of singing), while others discover various means of developing and sharing their musical interests (e.g., dancing with their infant to the parents' favorite dance music). In short, parents are exposed to various musical options and are encouraged to pursue music in a personally meaningful manner.

Unlike music programs for older children, there are no relevant standards or guidelines for programs involving infants or toddlers. In view of the interesting musical environment that mothers often provide for their infants, it is unclear whether such programs are necessary or desirable in the first year of life. Nevertheless, more and more of these programs are appearing. Thus, the time is ripe for considering their pros and cons and engaging in serious reflection on the musical activities that are appropriate for infants, toddlers, and their parents. See the author's Web site for suggestions of developmentally appropriate experiences.

5
foundations:
Developmentally
Appropriate Practice

Developmentally Appropriate Practice

There is no single accepted theory in child development, probably because development and learning are so complex that no present theory is adequate to explain these phenomena. There are, however, principles that inform practice. The broad-based review of the literature on early childhood education by the The National Association for the Education of Young Children generates three dimensions of information or knowledge for developmentally appropriate practices and a set of principles to inform early childhood practice. Developmentally appropriate practice is an extremely important concept.

1. *What is known about child development and learning*—knowledge of age-related human characteristics that permits general predictions within an age range about what activities, materials, interactions, or experiences will be safe, healthy, interesting, achievable, and also challenging to children.
2. *What is known about the strengths, interests, and needs of each individual child in the group*—the ability to adapt for and be responsive to inevitable individual variation.
3. *What is known about the social and cultural contexts in which children live*—ensuring that learning experiences are meaningful, relevant, and respectful for the participating children and their families (NAEYC, 1997).

Developmental Principles

National Association for the Education of Young Children

The NAEYC lists twelve empirically based principles of child development and learning that inform practice. The following italicized list resulted from a broad-based review of the early childhood literature (NAEYC, 1997). Musical examples are added to the NAEYC's principles.

1. *Domains of children's development—physical, social, emotional, and cognitive—are closely related. Development in one domain influences and is influenced by development in other domains.* Music touches several domains of children's development, for example, music singing game involves domains of the physical (movement), social (group in a circle), and emotional (expressive import of music). The cognitive domain occurs in games such as *Cuckoo, Where Are You?* (author's Web site), in which the child is required to deduce where the cuckoo is hidden.

2. *Development occurs in a relatively orderly sequence, with later abilities, skills, and knowledge building on those already acquired. Human development research indicates that relatively stable, predictable sequences of growth and change occur in children during the first nine years of life.* The relatively orderly sequence helps with organizing and planning experiences for children. Basic musical understandings such as faster/slower or louder/softer belong in the early childhood curriculum and need to be mastered as a foundation to later musical abilities.

3. *Development proceeds at varying rates from child to child as well as unevenly within different areas of each child's functioning. Each child is a unique person with an individual pattern and timing of growth, as well as individual personality, temperament, learning style, and experiential and family background.*

4. *Early experiences have both cumulative and delayed effects on individual children's development; optimal periods exist for certain types of development and learning.* An **optimal** period refers to those periods in which development will be faster or easier. For example, it is easier to learn to sing in tune during the ages of three to six years than at twenty-five to twenty-eight years of age. Maria Montessori wrote about **sensitive periods** when a child may learn specific skills more easily. Authors often confuse optimal periods with **critical** periods. An optimal period refers to those periods in which development will be faster or easier. Critical period is defined those time frames in which there will be no development or stunted development if requisite stimulation is not present (Flohr and Hodges, 2002).

5. *Development proceeds in predictable directions toward greater complexity, organization, and internalization.* Learning in music proceeds from what Bruner called enactive (concrete) learning to symbolic or representational knowledge (Boardman, 1988a, 1989; Bruner, 1983). Developmentally appropriate music programs provide a variety of musical experiences in which the children are actively engaged in music. Gradually children are helped to acquire symbolic knowledge through representation of their experiences in improvising, creating, dramatic play, and pre-music reading experiences such as moving their hands to show the contour of the music.

6. *Development and learning occur in and are influenced by multiple social and cultural contexts. Development is best understood within the sociocultural context of the family, educational setting, community, and broader society.* For example, a child in a musically rich home may be negatively affected by an educational setting with no music in the curriculum. Young children are influenced by the pop music culture in the society. Because culture is often discussed along with diversity or multiculturalism, parents and teachers often do not recognize the powerful role that culture plays in influencing the musical development of all children.

7. *Children are active learners, drawing on direct physical and social experience as well as culturally transmitted knowledge to construct their own understandings of the world around them.* These ideas support the use of music centers, and free music exploration (Chapter 10) where children are free to form their own hypotheses and try them out through physical manipulation of sound sources and through social interaction.

8. *Development and learning result from interaction of biological maturation and the environment, which includes both the physical and social worlds that children live in.* Nelson and Bloom cite numerous demonstrations that show how positive or negative early experiences can alter both the structure and function of the brain (Nelson and Bloom, 1997). Also, it is important to remember that a child's brain is not the same as an adult brain. During the first decade of life a child typically has up to twice as much neural activity and connections as adults. The brain makes connections during the prenatal period and throughout life. Some connections are predetermined genetically, and others develop from environmental influences (Flohr and Hodges, 2002). Chapter 9 examines the interaction between the anatomy of the child voice and the environment.

9. *Play is an important vehicle for children's social, emotional, and cognitive development, as well as a reflection of their development. When teachers provide a thematic organization for play; offer appropriate props, space, and time; and become involved in the play by extending and elaborating on children's ideas, children's language and literacy skills can be enhanced.* Organize the day and the environment for music play. Sociodramatic play for three- to six-year-old children is addressed in storytelling and dramatizing with music (author's Web site). Music centers filled with sound sources offer children an opportunity for play. Also, music singing games may be used for group play. For a summary on play, see Morrison's *Early Childhood Education Today* (Morrison, 1998).

10. *Development advances when children have opportunities to practice newly acquired skills as well as when they experience a challenge just*

beyond the level of their present mastery. Moreover, in a task just beyond the child's independent reach, the adult and more-competent peers contribute significantly to development by providing the support-ive **scaffolding** *that allows the child to take the next step.* Best practices include minimizing the chance of repeated failure and giving children a chance to practice musical skills. The techniques of free and guided exploration help children practice acquired skills and challenge them to move beyond their present level.

11. *Children demonstrate different modes of knowing and learning and dif-ferent ways of representing what they know. The principle of diverse modalities implies that teachers should provide not only opportunities for individual children to capitalize on their strengths but also opportu-nities to help children develop in the modes or intelligences in which they may not be as strong.* A common technique in music education is to ask children to sing, to watch the teacher move, and then to move their own arms to show the contour of the music thereby engaging the auditory, kinesthetic, and visual sense modalities. Music experiences are capable of addressing several of Gardner's intelligences including, musical, spatial, bodily-kinesthetic, intrapersonal, interpersonal, lin-guistic, and logical-mathematical.

12. *Children develop and learn best in the context of a community where they are safe and valued, their physical needs are met, and they feel psychologically secure. In addition, children's development in all areas is influenced by their ability to establish and maintain a limited number of positive, consistent primary relationships with adults and other chil-dren.* Music experiences in a secure classroom setting address social and emotional needs of children. A good example of how music experi-ences nurture social needs is found in singing games. As the children play a game such as *The Mill Wheel* (author's Web site) they engage in a community where everyone forms a circle and moves together as they pretend to grind corn. As children engage in singing, moving, and play-ing instruments together, they form a musical community. This musical community is a powerful force in the lives of children. High school graduates often speak of their musical community in statements such as, "If it were not for band, I don't know what might have happened to me in high school."

MENC beliefs about young children

In addition to the twelve NAEYC principles, MENC lists ten "beliefs" about young children designed to guide decisions about developmentally appropriate practice (MENC, 1991). Reprinted with permission. For example, All children have musical potential. Every child has the poential for successful, meaningful interactions with music. The development of these potentials, through numerous encounters with a wide variety of music and abundant opportunities to participate regularly in developmentally appropriate music activities, is the right of every young child. Visit www.menc.com for the complete list.

Summary and Key Points

Below are key points about developmentally appropriate practice to consider.

1. Individual children are unique, there is great variation among children's development. As they grow past the basic developmental milestones of the first year or two, the environment along with the child's unique genetics begin to influence a wider range of individuality.
2. Development and learning are complex and a single theory has not been accepted to explain the phenomena.
3. Children develop in a cultural, social, and historical context. Different cultures, periods of history, social classes, and racial/ethnic groups combine to affect development.
4. Belief in the idea of music aptitude as inherited or teachable affects the way the teacher instructs and the parent raises the child. There are critical and optimal periods when experiences may affect later development.
5. For a child to achieve a musical skill such as keeping the steady beat, many experiences are needed to practice and develop the skill. The beginning experiences should be easy to attain and subsequent experiences more difficult. However, individual children may differ in their skill. One child may perform the steady beat (to the standard of performance) on the first experience. Others may take five days of different experiences before they have the skill to keep the steady beat. Others may need twenty-five experiences over the course of one or two years.

6

Methods and Organization: Methods

Introduction

There are many ways to teach young children. The choices are affected by teaching skills, preferences, and individual learning differences in children. Each individual teacher must decide which method to use. A teacher may decide to specialize in one particular method or combine ideas from several methods.

Methods do not stand apart from history and there are historical relationships among the methods and educational thought. For example, Pestalozzi contributed ideas of sequence, repetition, and rote learning during the nineteenth century. An influential figure in American education, Lowell Mason, understood the value of Pestalozzi's work and Pestalozzi's ideas permeates many of the methods. The oldest method examined here is that of Emile Jaques-Dalcroze, who in turn influenced both Montessori and Orff. Kodály incorporated techniques from many sources including the solfège ideas of Glover and Curwen.

A method includes many suggested experiences and provides a systematic and/or sequenced plan for achieving objectives and/or goals. A method consisting of several experiences is not a curriculum unless organized as a curriculum with sequence, objectives and/or goals, learning and development theory, and philosophy. What is a musical experience? For example, clapping the steady beat to music is an activity. When an objective is linked to clapping of the steady beat such as "the child will synchronize his/her clapping to steady music of one hundred beats per minute," the activity becomes an experience. Experiences are teaching activities or strategies that are linked to an objective. Recall, in Figure 1.3, how many experiences (the leaves) grow out of method.

All methods do not have the same degree of organization or body of pedagogy and proponents of methods often prefer to refer to the method as a process or technique. The Kodály method or process, for example, is based on the idea that all children can be musically literate and Kodály pedagogy is sequenced to achieve specific literacy objectives.

Firsthand knowledge of any method is essential before enrolling in training or enrolling a child in a class. After watching a demonstration class of a method a teacher or parent may decide to look further.

Traditional Methods

The traditional methods (reviewed in this chapter) were all developed before 1960 but continue to be used. These methods created by Dalcroze, Montessori, Orff, Kodály, music series books, and Suzuki are presented in chronological order.

Table 6.1 gives an overview of the methods. Five topic descriptors are used in Table 6.1. **Fundamental idea** refers to the philosophy and/or basic idea of the approach. **Instructional goal** refers to the overall program goal. **Primary musical vehicle** refers to the way(s) in which the child experiences music. **Teacher skills** refer to musical skills emphasized in the method. Traditional and other methods require all or most of the following teacher skills: an accurate, expressive, and pleasant singing voice; ability to lead movement and dancing activities; knowledge about music and movement development; ability to share songs and rhymes from memory; and ability to be personable and comfortable with both children and adults. **Training** gives a brief overview of the types of training available. Table 6.2 (author's Web site) summarizes what a four-year-old would be expected to do in each method.

Dalcroze

Emile Jaques-Dalcroze (1865–1950) believed that humans feel emotions by various sensations produced at different levels of muscular contraction and relaxation. Abramson explains that human emotions are translated into musical motion, the emotions are sensed in various parts of the body and are felt by the various levels of muscular contraction and relaxation (Choksy, Abramson, Gillespie, Woods, and York, 2001). Human emotion's contraction and relaxation moves in a way analogous to the way in which the tension and release of music moves. Both emotion and music are related to movement.

The child's ear and body are the primary focus of instruction. While teaching at a conservatory Dalcroze found that many of his students could perform music technically but their performances were devoid of musical feeling and expression. He spent the rest of his life developing ways to help his students play musically. Dalcroze believed that a child should be able to express what is heard through movement before translating her/his physical sensations through singing, playing, creating. The entire Dalcroze method includes not only eurhythmics but also improvisation and solfège. Dalcroze categorized rhythmic performance into three types (Caldwell, 1992). **Arhythmic** performance is spastic and offbeat. **Errhythmic** performance has all the notes in the right place but is dull and boring with no nuance of weight, motion, and time. **Eurhythmic** performance balances motion and rhythm and make-the-music move so that the audience and performer are emotionally moved. To perform in a **eurhythmic** way, the musician must be able to control her/his performance in an **errhythmic**, synchronized way. Dalcroze saw the link between mind and body and how he might guide students to expressive music by involving them in movement experiences.

Table 6.1   Methods for Teaching Music to Young Children

METHOD	FUNDAMENTAL IDEA	INSTRUCTIONAL GOAL	PRIMARY MUSICAL VEHICLE	TEACHER SKILLS	TRAINING
Feierabend	Promoting appropriate child development in music & movement from birth to age 7 using American folk songs/ rhymes & classical music.	Nurture the music intelligence in all children so they can think tunes, feel the beat & rhythm, & respond to expressiveness in music.	Singing, moving & listening to American folk songs & rhymes, & moving with classical music	Pleasant singing voice; able to move comfortably. Expressive; sensitive; interpersonal skills for children/parents.	One week graduate summer class.
Fox–Eastman School	Music is play behavior. Based on play theories. Music experiences for families and children.	Child & parent learn about music through play. Four levels: 4 month–2 years, 2–3.5 yrs, 3.5–4 yrs, 5–6 yrs.	Singing & movement, 3–6 year olds use instrument and visiting musicians.	4-year college degree. Sing with confidence and lead children & adults in singing.	University courses and/or apprenticeship.
Gordon	Based on Gordon's music learning theory using eight-step process (birth through elementary age and above).	Audiation. Sound before symbol. Tonal and rhythm hearing & performance.	Listening, reading, singing.	Singing & rhythmic sense. Tonal & rhythm patterns from *Jump Right In!*	University courses.
Jaques-Dalcroze	Emphasis on rhythmically musical performance. For every musical sound there is a movement gesture. Preschool through college.	Good rhythm (eurhythmic) & ear training. Improvisation. Musical expression.	Improvisation & movement.	Improvisation. Piano skills or 2nd best, percussion or other instruments.	Intensive. Several courses & levels.
Harmony Road	Singing/piano based musicianship program (18 months–10 years).	Piano, inner hearing, improvisations, fixed do solfège.	Singing, piano, & movement.	Piano, vocal, improvisation skills. Must pass company training.	Company training.
Kindermusik	Music & movement program based on the belief that every child is musical. Birth–7 explore & discover.	Nurture the cognitive, emotional, language, social, physical, & musical development.	Movement, listening, vocal development, literacy, language-group performance	Singing. Company training.	2-3 day courses. 30 hr. Internet course.
Kodály	Music literacy for all children (birth–upper elementary).	Music literacy.	Singing (usually a cappella). Moving with hand signals.	Singing & ear training.	Intensive. Courses & levels.

Note: Methods are listed alphabetically. The table is not meant to be an exhaustive listing of all methods. Columns contain generalizations and are designed to give the reader a broad and general overview. The particular teacher using the method may change the focus. For example an Orff teacher may modify the method by using singing rather than mallet instruments as the primary musical vehicle. For more detail on each please consult references.

Table 6.1 Continued

METHOD	FUNDAMENTAL IDEA	INSTRUCTIONAL GOAL	PRIMARY MUSICAL VEHICLE	TEACHER SKILLS	TRAINING
MMCP	Development of a sequential music program emphasizing creating (early childhood–18).	Experiences help children manipulate sounds like a composer, performer, and conductor.	Creating.	Laboratory-type classroom. Centers for sound manipulation. Teacher is guide.	Publication only.
Montessori	Self-directed learning through sensory experience with teacher prepared materials (preschool–high school). Music integrated into total educational program.	Materials for pitch discrimination, vocal training, listening, pulse of music.	Sensory experiences with materials, singing, moving.	Teacher provides environment and uses questions to help student discover.	Intensive certification for total educational program.
Music Series Books	Curriculum for preschool-elementary & beyond (K–8+).	Objectives by grade level. Resource & curriculum for public school teachers.	Singing, listening, and creating, moving, reading/writing.	Assumes teacher can follow lessons and implement curriculum.	Offered by publishers.
Music Together	Highest quality music & movement experiences in parent/child classes. All children are musical (birth–preschool).	Playful, developmentally appropriate, nonperformance-oriented learning environment.	Learning through play. Singing, rhythm, movement.	Evaluation on tonal, movement & rhythm competency. Lead a class & lesson plans.	3–4 day.
Musikgarten	Enables teachers to understand how children from birth to age 9 learn music.	Help a child grow musically, emotionally, socially & cognitively.	Singing, moving, playing simple percussion.	Basic tonal & rhythmic competency.	15–18 hrs for each workshop.
Orff	Teach music to follow historic development. Start with chant & simple rhythm instruments (preschool–upper elementary).	Improvisation. Create music.	Percussive instruments; mallet instruments. Voice is secondary.	Rhythm, singing, & percussion instrument competency.	Intensive. Courses & certification levels.
Richards Institute ETM	Development of the child's total intelligence through a unique study of song through movement and play (preschool–age 12).	Immerse the child in song/play experiences. Goals for learning all subjects	Singing, moving and other experiences wrapped in play.	Strong play life, ETM song literature.	Several locations. 4+ weekends.
Suzuki	Humanitarian education & personality development, talent education (3 years–adult).	Performance skills and ear training.	Violin, viola, cello, bass, piano, flute, guitar, harp, recorder.	Violin (piano). Group instrumental lessons for beginners.	Intensive. Levels for certification.
Weikart	Movement is the base for music development & general development preschool–high school).	Feeling and expressing beat. Basic timing skills (steady beat).	Key movement experiences, e.g., describing.	Competency tests for trainer programs. No competency for 5-day.	Overview–5 day. Certification & endorsement.

Sample Dalcroze experience—Running and walking tempo. One experience involving movement would have the children walk around the room while the teacher improvises on the piano or a percussion instrument to match the general or average walking tempo of the children. The children learn to stop when the music stops. The teacher says "Get ready to stop," stops playing the piano and says "Stop." The same procedure is used to find the general or average running tempo for the children. Introduce a song at a walking tempo, such as *Twinkle, Twinkle, Little Star,* and encourage the children to sing the song in the children's walking tempo (while standing still). Ask the children to walk their hands over their body while the song is played at the walking tempo. The same strategy is used for the running tempo (being careful that the children run in a space with no obstacles). For more ideas, see Abramson (1973, 1998) and Caldwell (1992).

Montessori

Dr. Maria Montessori (see Chapter 2), like Dalcroze, believed the best way for children to learn is by doing. The most well-known musical aspects of Montessori's method are the instruments, such as wooden cylinders and the monochord for children less than five years of age. Six wooden cylinders are used to develop child's listening skills, compare sounds, match sound, and study dynamics. A teacher or parent can make cylinders or purchase or construct objects so that three sets have the same sound-making material inside. For example, find six same-colored plastic eggs and fill two with beans, two with sand, and two with small rocks. The only difference in the eggs is the sound they make as the child shakes them. As the child plays with the eggs, he/she will begin to categorize them by sound. The Montessori monochord looks like a small dulcimer with one string and is used to experiment with vibration (a child can see the string moving) and the way in which placing the finger on the instrument to shorten the string affects pitch. For children five years and older, Anna Maria Maccheroni, Montessori's music consultant, developed a double series of thirteen bells that are known as mushroom bells. The bells are used to teach pitch discrimination by matching and sorting the double set of bells.

Sample Montessori experience—Lesson of silence. Montessori's lesson of silence is an effective technique to prepare children for listening. She realized that to learn, the children needed to be very attentive listeners. The children listen to the sounds in the classroom during a count of ten (it is sometimes helpful to hold up ten fingers and one by one silently lower them for the count). Then ask the children what they heard. For example, a child may have heard an air conditioner, a bird, or a siren. Another child may have heard someone talking in the hall. Oftentimes, children will make up something they heard such as, "I heard a caterpillar crawling on a leaf." Use the lesson of silence to prepare the children to carefully and attentively listen to music.

Orff

Carl Orff (1895–1982) was a German composer who developed a method to enrich children's lives through cultivating their inherent musicality (Frazee and Krewter, 1987). The Orff method combines children's love of music making and love of sound with the child's need to participate in their own music education and personal growth.

The German term *Schulwerk* is often associated with Orff's music education method. "*Schulwerk* is an indication of the educational process taking place: *Schulwerk* is schooling (in music) through working, that is, through being active and creative" (American Orff-*Schulwerk* Association, 2003). Musical growth is fostered by experiences in performing (speech/chant, singing, playing), moving, listening, and improvising. Music is always connected to movement, dance, and speech.

A hallmark of the method is the use of rhythm instruments and melody instruments that can be immediately played by children. Special melody instruments, similar to standard xylophones and glockenspiels, were developed in the 1920s and have become known as Orff instruments. Other instruments for playing and improvising include recorders, unpitched percussion, voice and body. Orff instruction is built on a four-stage learning process of imitation, exploration, literacy, and improvisation (Frazee and Krewter, 1987). Imitation is simultaneous imitation, remembered imitation (echo imitation), and overlapping imitation. Orff thought early instruction that emphasized music reading was a cause of unmusical learning, and that the symbols of notation and music reading should only come after the children learn to speak in music by improvising and performing—the sound before the symbol.

Another feature of the Orff method is elemental style, that makes use of ostinati, bordun, pentatonic scales, and layering of sound. The ostinato may be a repeated simple movement such as alternating patting the legs and clapping the hands, a speech pattern, a melodic pattern (sung), or an instrumental pattern. A common technique to produce elemental style is to layer ostinati. The basic texts of *Schulwerk Music for Children (Volumes 1-5),* provide models for teachers, and these models have been adapted in many countries to include traditional music and folklore of each country (Orff and Keetman, 1950–54).

Sample Orff Experience—Improvisation on Are You Sleeping?   Children experience playing instruments and improvising in this Orff experience. First sing the song *Are You Sleeping?* Then layer the sounds, one child at a time. Begin with the bass xylophone, add the alto xylophone, add the wood block, add the finger cymbals and finally sing the song. Sing and play the song *Are You Sleeping?* and offer the children, one at a time, the opportunity to improvise their own music on another xylophone (remove bars to build a gapped pentatonic or five-tone scale: pitches f, g, a, c, and d are present) or rhythm instrument for the same time duration as the song. Give all the children a turn playing the xylophones, woodblock, and finger cymbals as well as a turn to improvise.

American folk song/arr. JWF

Figure 6.1 *Are You Sleeping?*

General Music Series Textbooks

The roots of American music textbooks began over one hundred years ago with singing books and public education. The chronological placement of the texts is difficult, but they have been part of American schools for many years. Each series is an effort to build a curriculum often combining several methods with sequenced experiences. Each series text usually includes teacher manuals with lesson plans, recordings, attention to special education, connections to other subjects, and multicultural music. The series texts usually have a kindergarten text. The kindergarten and first–second grade materials are often useable with three-year-olds and four-year-olds.

Kodály

What has become known as the Kodály method was developed by Zoltán Kodály (1882–1967) during the 1940s and 1950s. Kodály was a Hungarian composer, educator, and ethnomusicologist. Under his guidance, the practices of music education in Hungary gradually evolved and became famous throughout the world.

Kodály selected techniques and practices from a wide range of sources including a solfa approach from Italy, rhythm syllables from the French Chevé system, hand-signing from the British educator John Curwen, and a developmental approach based on the ideas of the Swiss educator Pestalozzi. Kodály's philosophy and the principles underlying the method are:

1. Music literacy is the primary means for musical independence.
2. Singing is the foundation for musicianship (*a cappella*—without accompaniment).
3. Use only the highest quality music either composed or folk.
4. Music experiences should begin early, in fact before the mother of the child is born!
5. Musical experiences should be grounded in the folk style of the culture; hence the term mother tongue, a term also used by Suzuki.
6. Music education should be available to everyone, not only the elite.
7. Use the moveable **do** solfège system.
8. Experiences come before notation.
9. The curriculum should be child-centered and music should be at the heart of the total curriculum and treated as a core subject.

The Kodály method is a highly structured and sequenced method with well-defined skill and concept taxonomies (Chapter 7) for the elements of music including rhythm, pitch, timbre (tone color), form, and dynamics and expressive devices. Its primary goal is music literacy for all children. The three basic tools of the Kodály method are tonic solfa, hand signs, and rhythm duration syllables. Moveable solfa is a system of syllables—**do, re, mi, fa, so, la, ti, do**—where the **do** is always the key or tonal center. This moveable **do** system contrasts with the fixed **do** system used by Dalcroze, in which **do** is always middle C. Kodály's adaptation of Curwen's hand signs was to reinforce tonal and visual memory of the solfa system. The technique involves using the hand in a different shape for each pitch (Figure 6.2).

The third major tool is rhythm duration syllables such as **ta** and **ti**. Several methods besides Kodály use rhythm syllables or mnemonics. For example, the rhythm pattern quarter, eighth, eighth would be **ta ti-ti** (Chapter 11).

In the Kodály method a Prepare—Present—Practice or Prepare—Make Conscious—Practice pattern is advocated. This instructional scaffolding technique is applicable to three- and four-year-old children. The idea is that before a concept such as the rhythm pattern, **ta ti-ti** (quarter, eighth-eighth) is taught, the children need to first be prepared by performing and hearing experiences that include the rhythm pattern. Next the child engages in music experiences (singing songs, playing games, listening, and playing instruments) that use the rhythm pattern. When the teacher introduces the notation symbols for the rhythm pattern, the child has experienced the sound of the rhythm pattern. The idea is then reinforced through practice of the notation symbols for the rhythm pattern.

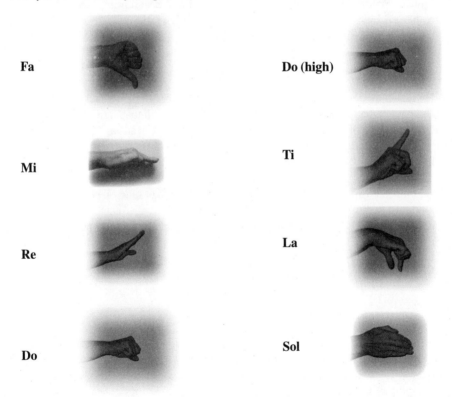

Figure 6.2 Hand Signs. Show children Do at waist level, move gradually up to Sol across from eyes and high Do above head.

Snail,   snail,   Snail,   Snail,   Creep   a - round and   'round and 'round.

Figure 6.3   *Snail, Snail*

Sample Kodály Experience—Snail, Snail

Singing games are productive for teaching singing to young children because they require much repetition. Based on folk music, they require repetitions of the song, often include movement, and are developmentally appropriate play experiences.

The Game

While singing the song the teacher makes a snail shell shape in the palm of the hand. Lay one hand palm up and with the forefinger of the other hand make a shape like Figure 6.4. For older children form a line with the children each holding one another's hands. The teacher leads the line and winds up in a coil like a snail shell and then unwinds. A small snail puppet is useful for this game.

Suzuki

The Suzuki method or **Talent Education** is named after Shinichi Suzuki (1898–1998). While in Germany studying violin, Suzuki's difficulty with the German language triggered his ideas of the mother tongue approach to music learning. Children learn to speak their mother tongue with ease; Suzuki developed his music method by mirroring the way children learn language. The method uses daily listening and imitation, constant repetition, praise, and encouragement in a positive nurturing home and lesson environment. Children as young as three years develop their musical ear before they are introduced to music reading just as children speak their mother language before learning how to read. Major success of the method is evident in group performances of Suzuki trained children (Morita, n.d.). The title of one of Suzuki's books, *Nurtured by Love*, underlines the importance of the nurturing environment (Suzuki, 1969).

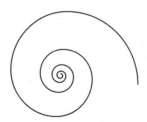

Figure 6.4   Snail, Snail

The major goal of the method is not to produce musical prodigies but, rather, to foster the development of the total child. Suzuki's method and its mother tongue technique differ from traditional methods of teaching instrumental music. Nine basic principles define the method. (1) Begin as early as possible. Suzuki recommended training or ability development to begin at birth. Formal training usually begins by age three. A parent must play the instrument around the home and the child decides on her own to play the instrument based on imitating the parent. (2) Teach in small steps so the child masters the material and feels a sense of success. Each child progresses at his/her own pace. (3) Either the mother or father attends all lessons in order to understand the learning process and objectives, and can work with the child as a home teacher. (4) The child listens daily to recordings of the Suzuki repertoire as well as to other music. (5) Postpone music reading until the child's aural and performance skills are well established in the same way children learn to read only after they can speak. (6) Follow Suzuki repertoire sequence (for the most part). It was designed and refined to produce the results that have come to be expected from the method. (7) Create an enjoyable learning environment so that the child will have enthusiasm for learning. (8) Group lessons and individual lessons are valuable. For the younger children the emphasis is often on group lessons. The parent(s) reinforce the lessons at home. (9) Foster the attitude of cooperation rather than competition among students.

Since the development of the Suzuki method many other methods incorporate his ideas. Although the method is traditionally instrumental, teachers in Finland have applied the ideas to vocal training (Matthews, 1991). The Suzuki method began with violin instruction but now includes teacher training and materials for violin, viola, cello, bass, piano, flute, guitar, harp, and recorder.

Contemporary Methods

There are probably as many instructional methods as there are teachers and not every teacher uses only one method. Each teacher often adapts, incorporates, and modifies ideas from a variety of methods. The term for this use of various ideas is eclecticism and new methods are normally built upon ideas from older methods. For example, Kodály was a true eclectic in th practices he used to formulate his ideas (but some teachers using his methods advocate eclecticism). Many methods designed after 1960 incorporate ideas from the traditional methods. Several methods produce commercially available materials and charge various fees for training and training leading to certification. Ellen Pollock, reporter for the *Wall Street Journal*, notes, "Forget about the nice music teacher in the basement down the street: Today's parents are sending their toddlers to national programs, some with slick handouts and even Web sites" (Pollock, 1999, p. 1). Some methods require a lesson fee per each student enrolled in classes. Lorna Heyge (founder of *Kindermusik*) in an interview about preschool music, comments about the commercialization, "It's just too bad if it [teaching music to children] just gets stuck in a trademark war" (Pollock, 1999, p. 4).

Review the tables and refer to the resource list at the end of the chapter for more information on contemporary methods.

Delivery models

There are at least six general models for delivering music instruction to young children. Models include (1) music instruction with the parent present including prenatal classes, (2) parent involvement in the home, (3) music taught to a group by a music specialist, (4) general music taught to a group by a classroom teacher, (5) individual child with a teacher, and (6) instrumental instruction. Each of these models is used as part of multiple methods. For example, many methods (e.g., Suzuki, Feierabend, Music Together) require parent support and presence at the lessons. Several of the methods such as Kodály or Dalcroze require a music specialist. Other methods such as Weikart's have been organized so that preschool, elementary, and physical education teachers do not require music training other than training in the method. The models often overlap; for example, the Suzuki method uses individual lessons and group activities with a parent present.

Choosing a Method

With so many choices, choosing one method for teaching music to young children is difficult. There are several issues to consider. Of first importance is, form a system of beliefs leading to a personal philosophy of music education. While the personal philosophy is in place, consider the follow key points before making a choice.

Summary and Key Points

1. The research studies on methods are not definitive. Which is better depends on the philosophy, students, situation, objectives, instructional approach to learning, as well as the teacher's training and perception. Comparing methods is like comparing apples to oranges. It is probably better to center thoughts on present instructional strategies rather than spending time deciding how some methods are bad and some methods are good.

2. Should a teacher concentrate on one method or use several methods? Method experts often think it best to choose one method. The authors of *Teaching Music in the Twenty-First Century* write "[N] o *combination* of methods can be as effective . . . as a knowledgeable use of any one of them in the hands of a teacher with sufficient training" (Choksy et al., 2001, p. 335.). Using techniques from more than one method may prove advantageous provided you have a clear philosophy of music education, link experiences with objectives, and organize experiences (see Chapter

7). If you use techniques from several methods, be sure to study those methods. Costanza and Russell (1992, p. 501) suggest that the most effective methods and experiences are those that the teacher knows best.

The various contexts of teacher-learner and the culture surrounding the delivery of music instruction make the selection of a single best practice virtually impossible. What may be possible is a list of promising practices, proven practices and, possibly, practices agreed to be best practices. Master teachers often identify principles of promising or best practices (Chapter 5) and combine the principles for use in their specific teaching situation. For example, the teacher may use Kodály principles to begin teaching rhythm and further develop rhythm by using Orff principles.

3. What is the teacher's level of musicianship? Some methods demand a much higher level of musicianship than others. For example, a certified Dalcroze teacher needs adequate improvisation and performance skills. A certified Kodály or Orff teacher, for example, must pass three levels of competency.

4. What is the amount of necessary training? Is a teacher willing to devote time, energy, and money to that training?

5. What are the ongoing costs? There are costs for materials, instruments, training, and also ongoing costs for licensing or cost per pupil and class.

6. How do the goals and vehicle for understanding music fit with the teacher's musical skills and beliefs? Visit a recommended teacher successfully using the method to be considered.

7. Does the method have curricula for the age of children you wish to teach? For example *Lovenotes* (Zemke, 1989) is designed for prenatal classes.

8. Consider the demands of the school district or teaching situation. Some school systems base their curriculum on one particular method.

9. Consider the cultural issues and values. For example, Kodály uses indigenous folk songs while other methods may use recently composed songs. Does the teacher, the school, or family value singing more than being able to play the piano or violin? Remember the NAEYC principle of child development. Development is best understood within the sociocultural context of the family, educational setting, community, and broader society.

10. Consider the individual differences among children. Some of the methods may readily accommodate special needs. For example, Orff, Kodály, Gordon, or Dalcroze may be used with handicapped individuals (Pinson, 2001).

11. In a sense all the various teaching methods can be divided into the categories of teacher-centered or student-centered methods (Colwell and

Wing, 2004). Is the method (or the way in which you are using the method) more child-centered or is it more teacher-centered? Current thinking in early childhood education advocates a child-centered approach.

Sources for Methods

Many of the methods and associations may be accessed through the World Wide Web.

Feierabend, books published by G.I.A. Publications (see below).

Fox–Eastman School, Donna Brink Fox, Ph.D., Eastman School of Music, 26 Gibbs Street, Rochester, NY 14604.

G.I.A. Publications-Music Series, 7404 South Mason Avenue, Chicago, IL 60638.

Gordon, Edwin E., G.I.A. Publications, Inc. (see above).

Harmony Road, Music Course, 17300 SE 82nd Dr., Clackamas, OR 97015.

Jaques-Dalcroze, Dalcroze Society of America, 2812 Fairmount Boulevard, Cleveland Heights, OH 44118-4020.

Kindermusik International, PO Box 26575, Greensboro, NC 27415.

Kodály—Organization of American Kodály Educators, 823 Old Westtown Road, West Chester, PA 19382.

Macmillan Music Series, Macmillan/McGraw-Hill, 1221 Avenue of the Americas, New York, NY 10020.

MMCP—Biasini, A., Thomas, R., & Pogonowski, L. (1970). *MMCP interaction: Early childhood music curriculum.* Bardonia, NY: Media Materials, Inc.

Montessori, American Montessori Society, 150 Fifth Avenue, New York, NY 10011.

Music Together, Center for Music and Young Children, 66 Witherspoon Street, Princeton, NY 08542.

Musikgarten, 507 Arlington Street, Greensboro, NC 27406.

Orff—American Orff-*Schulwerk* Association, P.O. Box 391089, Cleveland, OH 44139.

Richards Institute of Education Through Music ETM, 25702-C Holiday Circle, Stevenson Ranch, CA 91381.

Silver Burdett Making Music Series, Scott Foresman Company, (800) 552-2259.

Suzuki Association of the Americas, Inc., PO Box 17310, Boulder, CO 80308.

Warner Brothers Music Series, 15800 NW 48th Ave., Hialeah, FL 33014.

Weikart, High/Scope Educational Research Foundation, 600 N. River St., Ypsilanti, MI 48198-2898.

7
Methods and Organization: Organizing Instruction

A most important part of teaching is the organization of learning by teachers and parents. Organizing instruction on the basis of what activities to do today will not produce results as well as organizing instruction with objectives in mind. Better learning results when instruction is organized according to goals, and includes a clear idea of what the children can do at the moment and what you want them to be able to do at the end of the instruction periods (e.g., day, month, year).

Standards

The voluntary national standards are guidelines and there are no national standards inspectors visiting schools to check up on teachers (school district and state standards are often considered in teacher evaluation). The prekindergarten content standards are mainly targeted toward the four-year-old and younger (MENC lists ages two to four). Ages five through nine are included in the K–4 section. Prekindergarten content standards suggest experiences to include singing and playing instruments; creating music; responding to music (through movement); and understanding music understanding is used here to conform to the MENC standards [e.g., play instruments or verbalize to demonstrate awareness] (see MENC, 1994c, for more information).

Grades K–4 content standards include singing, alone and with others, a varied repertoire of music; performing on instruments, alone and with others, a varied repertoire of music; improvising melodies, variations, and accompaniments; composing and arranging music within specified guidelines; reading and notating music; listening to, analyzing, and describing music; evaluating music and music performances; understanding relationships between music, the other arts, and disciplines outside the arts; and understanding music in relation to history and culture (©MENC, 1994c). Reprinted with permission.

Objectives

Colwell and Wing (2004) define the basic objective of a school music program, from which all other objectives spring, to be the achievement of individual musical independence. Good music instruction uses clear objectives that can be assessed and the results acted upon for the next steps in instruction. It is important to distinguish between activities and experiences. Experience is purposeful, based on an objective or objectives, and has a definite form, while an activity may grow out of an experience but without an objective or evaluation. Activities are common and are useful, motivational, interesting, and enjoyable for children. For example, passing a ball around a circle to the beat of music is enjoyable. When ball-passing activity is linked to an objective and long-range plan for rhythmic development, it becomes an experience (refer to Colwell and Wing (2004), Chapter 4 for goals and objectives).

Taxonomies

Effective instruction arranges objectives in a sequence that leads to mastery. Sequencing comes in several forms. Learning proceeds from the concrete to abstract, from old to new, obvious to subtle, rote to note, short to long, single to multiple, part to whole, simple to complex, and familiar to unfamiliar (Colwell and Wing, 2004).

Colwell and Wing (2004) believe it is crucial for teachers to think about taxonomies. Taxonomies are helpful to classify, order, establish priorities or hierarchies, and to gain a reasonably complete idea of the scope of the field. Perhaps the most well-known taxonomy is Bloom's taxonomy. Table 7.1 illustrates a simplified taxonomy for young children's music learning based upon elements of music. Other taxonomies may be found in curriculum guides, series textbooks, and methods such as Kodály, Orff, and Dalcroze.

Objectives from any source need to be adjusted to the needs of individual students. For example, special education children need fewer objectives and more experiences.

Curriculum Design

A curriculum is a plan of instruction describing content (Colwell and Wing, 2004; Costanza and Russell, 1992). Curriculum guides are available from school districts, special programs, national and state programs. Two publications from MENC directly address early childhood (MENC, 1994c; Palmer and Sims, 1993). The important decision for every teacher is to choose or create the appropriate curriculum for her/his situation and children.

Evaluation of Student Learning

Evaluation is an overarching term used to describe judging or making value judgments about student, teacher, or program progress (Colwell, 1970). Evaluation includes assessment, testing, measurement, rubrics, data collection forms, parent reports, and portfolios (Boyle and Radocy, 1987; Brophy, 2000; Colwell, 2002a). Assessment is the "[C]ollection, analysis, interpretation, and application of information about student performance or program effectiveness in order to make education decisions" (Asmus, 1999, p. 21). The assessment may be **formative** or **summative**. Formative assessment is the feedback received that assists learning. Summative assessment is the judgment of whether an objective has been mastered to the target

Table 7.1   Taxonomy Example

RHYTHM

Level Concept
1. Music moves with a steady beat (heartbeat). Contrast with absence of steady beat.
2. Slower and faster beat.
3. One sound or rest can be concurrent with a beat (quarter note and quarter rest).
4. Sounds and rests through beat. Longer and shorter sounds.
5. Two sounds or rests to one beat (and combinations such as short-short-long, long short-short). There can also be more sounds on a beat (sixteenth notes).
6. Two and four beat durations (half and whole notes and rests).
7. Accents. Meter grouping of beat into two's and three's.
8. Sounds can be even or uneven.
9. Duple, triple, 6/8 meter (all part of our culture).
10. Accelerando and ritardando.

PITCH

Level Concept
1. Indefinite pitch. Exploration of sounds in environment.
2. Definite pitch.
3. Movement of pitches is melody (three-note melody). Melodies may move by steps, skips, or stay on the same pitch.
4. Pitches move up—pitches move down—pitches stay the same.
5. Higher-lower pitches.
6. Pentatonic melody.
7. Melody with tonal center; 7 pitch melodies.
8. Major/minor melodies.
9. Two or more pitches sounded together make harmony.

TIMBRE (TONE COLOR)

Level Concept
1. Expressiveness through timbre choice.
2. Contrast of timbre. You can change the sound of instruments depending on how you play them.
3. Combining timbre.
4. Percussion, brass, woodwind, string timbres.
5. Specific instrument timbres.

FORM

Level Concept
1. Overall form-expressive intent.
2. Repetition.
3. Contrast.
4. Unity, variety/variation. Phrase: Ability to sing in phrases rather than one or two notes at a time.
5. AB—two-part form.
6. Ostinato.
7. Introduction and coda.

Table 7.1   Continued

8. Rondo.
9. ABA—three-part form.

DYNAMICS & EXPRESSIVE DEVICES

Level Concept
1. Louder-softer. Forte (f) and piano (p).
2. Crescendo-diminuendo
3. Fortissimo (ff), pianissimo (pp), mp (mezzo piano).
4. Attack and release.
5. Shaping with dynamics.
6. The mood changes as the dynamics and rhythm change. Identify the emotional tone (e.g., sad or happy).

level of competence. In a developmentally appropriate curriculum both summative and formative assessments may be used to improve the teaching—learning environment. Authentic assessment is demonstrated performance during authentic, not contrived, activities. Accurate assessment of young children is difficult because children change rapidly, change in an uneven manner, and often exhibit episodic behaviors. For example, test-retest measures are often unreliable for children below the age of five years. The NAEYC outlines eight major guidelines for developmentally appropriate assessment practices.

1. Assessment of young children's progress and achievements is ongoing, strategic, and purposeful. The results of assessment are used to meet the developmental and learning needs of children.
2. The content of assessments reflects progress toward important learning and developmental goals. A systematic plan for collecting and using assessment information is integrated with curriculum planning.
3. The methods of assessment are appropriate to the age and experiences of young children. Therefore, assessment of young children relies heavily on the results of observations of children's development, descriptive data, collections of representative work by children, and demonstrated performance during authentic, not contrived, activities.
4. Assessments are tailored to a specific purpose and used only for the purpose for which they have been demonstrated to produce reliable, valid information.
5. Decisions that have a major impact on children, such as enrollment or placement, are always based on multiple sources of relevant information, particularly observations by teachers and parents.
6. To identify children who have special learning or developmental needs and to plan appropriate curriculum and teaching for them, developmental assessments and observations are used.

7. Assessment recognizes individual variation in learners and allows for differences in styles and rates of learning. Assessment takes into consideration such factors as the child's facility in English, and whether the child has had an opportunity to develop proficiency in his or her home language as well as in English.
8. Assessment legitimately addresses not only what children can do independently but also what they can do with assistance from other children or adults.

Issues

A difficulty in the summative assessment of young children involves performance standards and best or promising practices for children. Remember that summative assessment is judgment of whether an objective has been mastered to the target level of competence. There are three major problems.

First, children develop musical skills and concepts at different and individual paces. Some children can match pitch when they are two years old, others are not able to do so until age seven, and some have difficulty with matching pitch at fourteen years of age.

Second, the research base is not sufficiently broad to inform us about what children can achieve and at what age they are able to achieve. How many four-year-olds are able to identify a change from loud to soft in music? How many five-year-olds are able to clap the steady beat at 120 bpm? At present there are no answers to such questions, only bits and pieces of information.

Third, one of the beliefs of MENC is: *Prekindergarten children should not be encumbered with the need to meet performance goals. Opportunities should be available for children to develop accurate singing, rhythmic responses to music, and performance skills on instruments. Each child's attainment of a predetermined performance level, however, is neither essential nor appropriate* (MENC, 1991). Young children need time to develop without pressure to achieve set goals. So where does it leave teachers? At this time, the best a teacher can do includes using clear objectives, formative and summative assessment, little or no pressure on children to achieve performance goals, and general milestones of musical development.

Strategies for Assessment—Performance Standards from MENC

MENC offers several publications on assessment for children (Lehman et al., 1996; MENC, 1994b, 1994c; Sims, 1995). *The Performance Standards for Music Grades preK–12* contain specific strategies for assessing each of the content and performance (or achievement) standards. The strategies are divided into a prekindergarten (age two to four) and grades K–4 section. The assessment description is divided into three levels of achievement; basic, proficient, and advanced. Many examples for prekindergarten and grades K–4 are outlined in the document (Lehman et al., 1996, pp. 19–60). Table 7.2 is an example of a prekindergarten (ages two to four) assessment (Lehman et al., 1996, p. 19).

Table 7.2   Prekindergarten Assessment of National Standard

CONTENT STANDARD:
1. Singing and playing instruments

ACHIEVEMENT STANDARD:
1a. Children use their voices expressively as they speak, chant, and sing

ASSESSMENT STRATEGY:
The teacher and the child chant a short, familiar poem together. The teacher then asks the child to try using different kinds of voices (e.g., high, low, funny, scary, whispery) in reciting the poem. The teacher invites the child to suggest other kinds of voices, and the child again chants the poem, using other kinds of voices.

DESCRIPTION OF RESPONSE:
Basic Level:
1. The child can offer a few suggestions, but the suggestions tend to be derived from the teacher's examples and reflect little originality.
2. The child is willing to try using the various kinds of voices, but the distinctions are minimal and unconvincing.

Proficient Level:
1. The children can demonstrate several kinds of voices that have not previously been suggested by the teacher. Some of the suggestions may be derived from the teacher's examples, but others are clearly original.
2. The child can offer a convincing demonstration of each kind of voice suggested.

Advanced Level:
1. The child can demonstrate a wide variety of voices that cover most of the possible categories. Many are clearly original. The child shows flexibility and imagination in demonstrating a wide variety of voices.

©MENC, 1996. Reprinted with permission.

Tracking Student Growth by Observation.   Much assessment of children is through teacher observation. Observation can be an efficient way to assess children and can streamline into the flow of the class period. As the children sing, play, move, create, and listen the teacher monitors and records the activity of individual children and groups of children. The concepts and skills in the curriculum or taxonomy are the basis for observation. Behaviors the teacher should observe include moving (show the way the music moves with hands and head), performing (sing the phrase or play the phrase), reading (read and clap the short pattern), writing (arrange flat wooden sticks to show the rhythm), creating (make up a new way to play the instrument), and listening (raise hand when you hear the trumpet). Systematic observation is recommended because anecdotal reports are casual observations or indications rather than rigorous analysis of important behaviors that are indicators of the child's developing musicality. Systematic observations are useful in many circumstances including behavior problems and may include frequency counts of behaviors, event sampling (recording an event each time it occurs), duration recording (how long does the behavior take), time sampling (how often the behavior occurs during a set time period) or analysis of **rehearsal frames** (the frame begins when the teacher identifies a skill or concept and ends when the objective is accomplished or when work on a new objective is begun) (Duke, 1999/2000).

Tracking Student Growth with Data Collection Forms and Rubrics. A teacher often has hundreds of children to teach each week. Data collection methods such as checklists and rating forms help streamline the assessment process and provide written data for sharing with parents, other teachers, and administrators. A rubric is a set of scoring criteria used to determine a child's performance on a task or concept. For example, in Table 7.2 the three levels of basic, proficient, and advanced were used to assess the child's response. Table 7.3 illustrates a slightly different way to assess responses using four achievement levels.

Table 7.4 is an example of a data collection form (multilevel rubric) designed to assess fundamental concepts for young children.

Portfolios. Portfolios are a popular way to collect data. Portfolios of observations, collections of representative work, and child performance during authentic activities are appropriate to the age and experiences of young children. A child's portfolio could include (1) videotape footage of common classroom experiences of performing, creating, and listening while moving to music; (2) observation rubrics noting development; (3) recordings of singing and playing instruments (children often love to sing for the microphone); and (4) writing or drawings in which the child has represented rhythms, instruments used in listening experiences, tonal movement, or musician guests and their instruments in the classroom.

Verbal Questions. Questions can help teachers learn what the children are thinking. Piaget made extensive use of listening to children and asking questions. Overt responses are assessable by many methods, but thoughts of children less than six

Table 7.3   Rubric for Playing Two Pitches Simultaneously in Rhythm on a Xylophone

ACHIEVEMENT	DESCRIPTION
Level 1	*novice:* plays without a steady beat for most of the time. The two pitches are not played simultaneously.
Level 2	*emerging/progressing:* plays with a steady beat for at least half the piece, but is sporadic.
Level 3	*accurate/competent:* plays the entire piece with the exception of 1–2 beats in rhythm and with both hands striking simultaneously.
Level 4	*outstanding/accomplished:* plays correctly for entire piece. Draws sound out of the xylophone. Performance is remarkable for age and/or prior experience.

Table 7.4   Sample Data Collection for Musical Skills/Concepts

NAME	EU	HL	LS	MU/D	SL	130	120	PT	OT	SD	SS
Dianne	m					e					
Joanne	e					m					
John			m								
Sandy	d										
Valerie								d			

ACHIEVEMENT KEY

M	Student has mastered the skill/concept
E	The skill/concept is emerging
N	Student needs more work on skill/concept
D	Difficulty with the skill/concept

CONCEPT KEY

EU	even-uneven
HL	higher-lower
LS	longer-shorter
MU/D	moving up-moving down
SD	same-different
SF	slower-faster
SL	softer-louder
SS	stop-start
130 bpm	steady beat
120 bpm, etc.	steady beat
PT	preferred beat
OT	other tempi

years of age are much more difficult to assess. For example, take the child who asks, "Why is the grass green?" The child will not accept an explanation of photosynthesis, sun, chlorophyll, and carbon dioxide. By using questions you find the child is thinking of a reason for green and will accept something like, "Because then the caterpillars can hide in the grass." Questions are particularly useful for finding out what the child may perceive, be listening to, or recognize in the music. Questions should be stimulating, easy enough for the child to answer, clear, and relevant to what is being studied at the time. Questions should usually not be answerable by "yes" or "no" or only asked of children who know the answer. For example, tap the rhythm pattern of the words to a song that was sung during the lesson (e.g., *Snail, Snail* from Chapter 6). Ask a child or the children to compare the pattern to another song, "Was that the way *Twinkle, Twinkle* sounds? Or the way *Snail, Snail* sounds?" After a child answers, clap the rhythm while singing the song to see if it fits the rhythm pattern.

Reports to Parents. The portfolio is particularly appropriate for reports to parents. Parents often find more meaning in a portfolio of their child's accomplishments than a percentage score of 81 percent on a test. Parents want to know when they should start their child on specialized instruction for instruments such as violin or piano (Flohr, 1987). A portfolio, rubric assessment, and standardized tests may all help the parent with information for an appropriate decision.

Assessment Criteria. For an assessment consider the following six criteria:

1. Consequences: Are they positive?
2. Fairness: Does it enable all children and children from all cultural backgrounds to demonstrate their achievement?
3. Generalization: Does the assessment adequately represent children? Are the results reliable and valid?
4. Cognitive complexity: Are higher levels of thinking addressed?
5. Content: Is the content consistent with what is known about music and learning? Is the curriculum's major points addressed? Is the assessment authentic and meaningful to everyone involved?
6. Cost/time: Are the outlay of funds and time worth the results?

Planning the Environment for Learning

Building an environment conducive to learning is not easy. There is no cookbook for teaching. Beginning teachers are sincere and want to do the best for children. An erroneous idea is that they will be the **magic** teacher who helps **any** child learn; who will take the most difficult situation and turn it around to save the child. The magic teacher is able to leap tall insurmountable learning problems in a single flick of an instructional finger! The reality is that many forces act upon children's learning (Colwell and Wing, 2004). Teaching is such a complicated enterprise that it is best viewed as an **art** and a **craft** rather than a set of techniques to apply as in following a cake recipe.

There are at least six general dimensions or ingredients to consider when organizing instruction. *First* are the child and the forces influencing the child. Current thought clearly supports a child-centered classroom with developmentally appropriate practice. But the child does not come to the classroom as a blank slate. Many forces influence a child including parents and other adults, emotional characteristics and the mood of the day, prior learning, how their needs are being met, and culture and the cultural context. The *second* ingredient is the teacher. The teacher brings to the situation a philosophy of music, beliefs about learning theory, knowledge of the subject, experience, emotional characteristics and mood for the day. *Third* is the environment, including temperature, weather patterns, physical space, safety, and equipment. *Fourth* is the social climate of the classroom and school. For example, what social interaction occurred in the last class? How does an individual child relate to other children as they engage in group music activities? *Fifth* is the instructional materials including lesson plans, instruments, methodology, and techniques. *Sixth* is the instructional moment. What are the forces in place at the moment and how does the teacher adapt the timing, sequence, and reinforcement of learning to best optimize all children's learning?

All six of the dimensions of instruction interact with each other. The teacher might wish to arrange a lesson so that a child will move from not being able to sing the pitches sol, mi, and la to the skill level of being able to sing those three pitches in tune, but learning is not necessarily a straight line. All the dimensions of instruction—the child, teacher, materials, social climate, instructional moment, and environment—interact with the singing objective. Figure 7.1 illustrates a simplified matrix of interaction for the dimensions of instruction. Each dimension such as social climate interacts with all other dimensions to influence the child's learning.

The Child

The more a teacher knows about a child, the better the teacher is able to help the child learn. The child's name (e.g., knowing the child's name or when other children have the same name), likes, dislikes, preferred mode of learning, stability of temperament, emotions, disposition to learning, siblings, parents, needs for attention, assessed

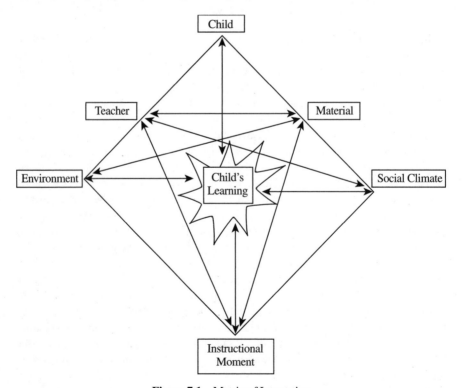

Figure 7.1 Matrix of Interaction

music skills and concepts, all interact with instruction. In a multidimensional society, the concepts of multiculturalism and special education are important to consider.

Special Education. Over thirty years ago parents and public officials designed legislation to give quality education to children with special needs. For the purposes of this brief overview, broad issues and terms are addressed including public law (PL) 94–142, least restrictive environment (LRE), individual educational program (IEP), mainstreaming, inclusion, and exceptional children. The Individuals with Disabilities Education Act (IDEA) of 1990 redefined disability as a physical or mental impairment that limits major life activities. Passage and implementation of PL 94–142, the Education for All Handicapped Children Act of 1975, mandated students with all types of disabilities be educated in the LRE, meaning that their education would be as close to normal as possible while offering specialized instructional support. Exceptional children include children with mental retardation, hearing problems, learning disabilities (such as ADHD, attention deficient disorder), behavior disorders, autism, visual, abused children, speech and language impairments, at risk, and other disabilities (such as orthopedically impaired, multihandicapped) as well as the gifted and talented. An IEP is a program designed specifically for one child to meet that child's needs. Music teachers are sometimes, but not often enough, asked to be part of the IEP team that analyzes the child's needs, determines objectives, and organizes instruction.

A specialized field of music, music therapy, exists to address the ways in which music aids children with special needs. Music therapy is available for young children and often available through the public schools for children through age twenty-one. Music therapists work with disabilities in four primary areas of motor, communication, cognitive, and social/emotional skills (Patterson, 2003; Pinson, 2002).

Mainstreaming and inclusion are terms referring to integrating the disabled or exceptional learners with non-disabled learners. "[M]ainstreaming, integration, and inclusion refers to the placement of children with disabilities into general music education settings" (Wilson, 1996, p. 334). In preschools children are normally included in the mainstream since many children who will later become identified as disabled are often not so identified during the preschool years. There are several good reasons and positive outcomes from inclusion including music's ability to reach children in a nonverbal way, providing social interaction with children from the entire school, and a single experience in music can be adapted for a wide range of abilities.

The Environment

The importance of the environment in learning and child development promoted by theorists such as Vygotsky and Bronfenbrenner is not a controversial idea. The parent and teacher are responsible for setting the best possible environment for the child's learning. A child-centered environment is preferred by the NAEYC to a teacher-centered environment. Teacher-centered refers to an environment in which the teacher is the leader and directs the activities. A child-centered instructional setting is one where the emphasis is on where the child is, their development, and developmentally appropriate practices.

The Teacher, Materials, Social Setting, and the Instructional Moment

The teacher, materials, and the social setting are significant components of the instructional setting. MENC lists several instructional components for prekindergarten including (1) instruction is provided by teachers with formal training in early childhood music and a qualified early-childhood music specialist is available as a consultant; (2) each room has high-quality sound production systems, parts of which may be operated by children; (3) each room has sound recordings representing a wide variety of music styles and cultures; (4) other equipment such as video cameras, VCRs, and multimedia equipment are available; (5) each room is equipped with appropriate classroom instruments; (6) adaptive devices are available for children with disabilities; and (7) each room is equipped with children's books containing songs and other music instructional materials (MENC, 1994c, pp. 1–2) (standards for elementary school children grades K–12 are listed in the same document).

During each instructional moment, the teacher makes decisions about how the lesson is progressing and implements changes that may help the children. The best-laid lesson plans may fail because of the interactions among instructional variables (Figure 7.1) and the poorly planned lesson may end well because the teacher takes a fresh look at the situation and adapts instruction. If there are six kindergarten classes during the week, how many lesson plans would be needed? Consider using one general lesson. In each class the teacher encounters different children, social climates, and environments. For each class the timing, pacing, and sequence will need to be adjusted. For one class moving from a hello song to a musical story may work well, but for another class (perhaps after recess), the hello song may best be followed by a movement activity. Only a novice teacher would stay on the predetermined lesson plan track as it begins to crash. The teacher needs to be flexible to the dynamics of the instructional moment and adapt the lesson to meet the children's developmental needs. Without flexibility, the plans may fail to produce learning or a satisfying lesson for the children.

Class Management and Motivation

Young children are naturally drawn to music. A teacher of young children does not need to sell music to children; the children love music and find it fascinating. Part of the teacher's (or parents) job is to utilize the child's intrinsic motivation to aid instruction.

Twenty Tools for Managing

1. Attend to the children. Learn their names as quickly as possible; knowing their names demonstrates that the teacher values the children and is

also useful for individual response. Saying, "Johnny, please keep your hands to yourself," is much more effective than "You in the blue shirt with yellow stripes, keep your hands to yourself."

2. Be consistent about boundaries, such as where to sit in the circle time, where the children are permitted, and personal boundaries for each child's space. Rules may be helpful, but young children will respond to action by the teacher rather than a list on the board. Keep as few rules as possible. There are many possibilities such as the three Bs, **"Be ready, Be respectful, Be responsible."**

3. Offer involvement in the activities to all children. Many adults still remember how they never were able to play the cymbal in first grade because their music teacher "didn't have time" or "forgot them." Competitive quasi-music games such as *Musical Chairs* are not appropriate. There should be no competition for an instrument.

4. Know the music and experiences thoroughly. The time to learn a new song is *not* when teaching young children.

5. Establish a way to pass out instruments and other materials, and a way to collect them.

6. Plan more experiences for the lesson than could possibly be done in the allotted time. One or more lesson items may be discontinued.

7. Have all the materials needed for class close at hand and in good working order.

8. Keep all activities moving swiftly, and be flexible. If there is dead space their contribution will often fill that space with unwanted behaviors. If a song or other activity is not working, go on to some other activity. Recognize when a movement activity is needed.

9. Do music rather than talk about music. Remember what the adults sound like on the Charley Brown shows? Something like, "Blah, blah, blah."

10. Be passionate about music. Passion for music is contagious.

11. Tell the children what they are to do. Do not ask them if they want to participate, especially two-year-olds because they love to say no. When a teacher asks children's opinions and then ignores a negative opinion the message is that the teacher does not value that opinion. Be careful not to reinforce children who are not achieving or behaving appropriately.

12. Stimulate children's learning by praising correct behavior and well-done experiences. For example, after a child performs a song well the teacher says, "Good, let's give her a hand," and begins clapping. Applause is part of the musical experience.

13. Create a good social climate by thanking the children for good performance or behavior. Do not give "thank you's" unless they are deserved.

14. Never compare children.

15. Be careful when offering children a choice, but offer a choice rather than dictating. For example, "Please play the instrument the way we learned or put it back in the bag."

16. Be flexible and consider changing the lesson sequence, pace, or timing.
17. Participating in and learning about music is intrinsically rewarding for young children. Extrinsic rewards are rarely appropriate.
18. Use repetition. Do not hesitate to repeat a song for several weeks or months. Children need much repetition to learn songs and other musical endeavors.
19. Use varied experiences. A thirty-minute lesson could be comprised only of singing, but a developmentally appropriate lesson usually uses several experiences and several avenues of music learning.
20. Bring attention-focusing materials and use attention-focusing techniques.

Attention Focusing Techniques. While young children are motivated to be active with musical experiences, they are easily distracted. A person walking into the room, a dog barking, a fire engine siren, any loud noise, a smell, or a myriad of other distractions easily move them off the task at hand. An important skill for anyone working with young children is the ability to focus children's attention. Following is a list of example focusing techniques.

1. *Surprise bag.* Bring a bag or box with a secret item each day or week. Ask a child (be sure to rotate turns) to help find the special surprise for the day. For example, when introducing a song such as *Twinkle, Twinkle,* the box would contain a small star or a star for each child.
2. *Listen to the sounds.* Listen to the sounds in the room while silently counting to ten (see Montessori section in Chapter 6).
3. *Finger plays.* Using finger plays focuses the child's attention on the chant or song and fine motor movement.
4. *Instruments.* A new instrument or an instrument not played for a few weeks will catch children's attention. Three-year-olds will even sit down and wait patiently in order to have a turn playing a maraca.
5. *Secret.* Young children respond with attention to, "I have a secret," or "The puppet has a secret." Simply hold a puppet to one ear and move the puppet's mouth. The secret could be anything needed at the time such as, "Ms. Kitty wants everyone to listen to this instrument sound."
6. *Interesting backup special activity.* Always have at least one interesting backup activity or item to gain attention. The item could be many things including a new electronic keyboard, a new rhythm instrument, or a puppet.
7. *Puppets.* Puppets are always good attention-getters. A puppet can help the children practice inner hearing. Ask the children to follow the puppet singing. "When the puppet has its mouth open, sing the song out loud. When the puppet has its mouth closed, think the song inside your head."
8. *Multisensory approach.* Use as many senses as possible to engage the child and keep their attention. Include hearing, seeing, and feeling. The senses of taste and smell are more difficult but possible to utilize.

9. *Anthropomorphisms.* Bring inanimate objects to life. For example say, "The piano is going to listen to you and watch you walk around the room. The piano will play some music that sounds like you move."

10. *Chant for attention.* Use a chant to draw attention. For example, say, "Ms. John-son, Ms. John-son," and then tap the rhythm on the floor, on the head, on the arm, and so forth. Another common example is the *Hear me chant.*

> If you hear me, put your finger on your head.
> If you hear me put your finger on your _____ (knee, floor)
> Continue using body parts and gradually get softer (diminuendo) and then,
> If you hear me, put your finger right here (and place finger on lips).

11. *Stories for attention span.* Storytelling with music is a proven way to gain and hold attention.

12. *Reinforce desired behavior.* Young children (less than six years) love attention from adults and relish compliments such as, "I like the way Christine is singing." Praise should be reserved for challenging work and not for ordinary expected behavior. Be careful not to reinforce groups of children or the entire class when all are not achieving or behavior in the appropriate manner. Dweck's work on student achievement and learner's perception indicates that parents and teachers should work toward convincing children that competence in a subject can be developed (Colwell and Wing, 2004; Dweck, 1999).

13. *Establish an archetypical model of correct behavior.* For example establish that a child needs to sit quietly before he will receive an instrument to play. Also, one word can serve to bring the children's attention to the model. **Supersinger** can be used to mean a child sitting in good singing posture, attentive, and on task.

Lesson Planning

A lesson plan form is useful when designing lessons for fifteen to twenty-five classes each week. Tables 7.6 and 7.7 offer a sample lesson placed into two formats. Table 7.6 is a sample kindergarten lesson plan form incorporating National Standards, Texas Assessment of Knowledge and Skill (TAKS), Texas Essential Knowledge and Skills (TEKS), Bloom's taxonomy levels, procedures, and assessment. Table 7.7 is a thumbnail sketch of the lesson that is useful for a less detailed view. The thumbnail system may be used to show an overview of weeks or months of lessons.

Lesson Components

Colwell and Wing (2004) list widely promoted lessons plan features summarized by Cruickshank, Bainer, and Metcalf.

Table 7.5   Kindergarten Lesson Plan

Objective-At the end of the lesson, the child will show when the music changes from soft to loud and loud to soft. With eyes closed, they will demonstrate their hearing of the change by raising their arm after the change occurs in the music.

National Standard Grades K-4: 6c, 6e

TEKS Objective(s) 4B: Identify louder/softer in musical performances.

TAKS Objectives-M2. The student will demonstrate an understanding of mathematical relations, functions, and other algebraic concepts.

Bloom's Level(s):
_x_Knowledge _x_Comprehension
_x_Application _Analysis
_x_Synthesis _Evaluation

Resources/Materials—CD of Haydn, *Surprise Symphony.* Any known song. Drums.
Set induction—Play Haydn's *Surprise Symphony* while the class enters. Identify loud and
   soft sounds in the classroom environment.
Methodology—**Play/create**: pass out drums. Demonstrate loud and soft on the drum.
   Encourage children to improvise new ways to play the drums loud and soft. **Listen**:
   listen to Haydn's *Surprise Symphony.* Find the very loud moment. **Move/create**:
   demonstrate and explore ways to move to Haydn. How can we show louder? **Sing**: sing
   a known song with very soft voices and loud voices (be careful not to encourage
   yelling). **Read**: use picture representation of loud and soft (e.g. a big wrapped gift and
   a small one). Draw a big **f** (forte) and a little **p** (piano)—the standard notation
   abbreviations for loud and soft.
Assessment—Observe the children as they use their arms to show when the music's sound
   level (dynamics) changes. Use Table 5.4 to collect data on achievement.
Closure—Sing goodbye song once softly and again loudly. Ask the children to leave softly.

Memos/special events:

Table 7.6   Thumbnail Sketch of Lesson

OBJECTIVE: Show when music is louder/softer.

NATIONAL STANDARD K-4: 6C, 6E
TEKS: 4B TAKS: M2

Induction: Play CD as they enter. Is it soft? Make a loud sound. Make a soft sound.

Materials: CD *Surprise Symphony,* drums.

Method: Play: drums/Listen: CD/Move: create/Sing: loud, soft/Read-icons and **f, p.**

Assessment: Use rubric, assess while they move.

Closure: Sing goodbye song **f** and **p.**

1. *Objectives*—Indicates the lesson's objectives.
2. *Resources*—Denotes resources and materials to be used.
3. *Set induction*—Describe how the lesson will be introduced.
4. *Methodology*—Describes how teaching and learning will take place.
5. *Assessment*—Makes clear how student learning will be determined.
6. *Closure*—Provides for lesson ending (Cruickshank, Bainer, and Metcalf, 1999, p. 149).

How to Plan: Preparing for the Children

One item that is usually lacking in teacher training is information about what to do the first day. This section is designed to prepare teachers of preschool and lower elementary school for the first day. The idea of what to do the first day has been expanded to several time frames.

What to Do before Beginning the First Music Class

All the materials must be in the classroom and available before beginning instruction. When working with children, all of the teacher's time should be given to the children. Following is a list of items to prepare.

If there is a music classroom, the following suggestions are appropriate.

1. Decorate the room with musical items. Keep the visually stimulating graphics on the sides and back of the room so that the visuals will not distract the children as they face the front for group instruction.
2. Create a sound exploration center with pictures of instruments, instruments, and sound sources.
3. Create a listening center with child operated CD/tape player.
4. Set the environment so that the children have a space for movement and circle time.
5. Obtain a good sound system. A wireless microphone with their sound system may be helpful.

The following suggestions are appropriate for all situations.

6. Contact the prior teacher and ask about the programs, problems, accomplishments, objectives, and experiences from past years.
7. Find out other teacher duties such as accompanist for school functions, director for plays, and leader for group singing.
8. Locate the school or school district curriculum. If none, locate the state guidelines or use the national standards.
9. If the teacher is traveling between rooms, she can make a box for each class to keep materials for each class. Take time to plan what instruments and materials to put on the cart.

10. Select an opening and closing song for the class to serve as a cue that music class is beginning or ending. The songs may be changed when the children have a repertoire of two class songs.
11. Many schools require that rules be announced and posted as well as consequences for unwanted behavior. Have a clear discipline plan. A folder for each child is helpful for keeping records about achievement and discipline.
12. Select recordings and/or songs for naptime and other set times in the day. Select songs to use for transitions. For example, choose a recording, perhaps *Flight of the Bumblebee,* to signal time to pick up toys.
13. Introduce yourself to school staff including teachers, new teachers, and janitors and establish good relationships. Remember janitors have all the keys.
14. Contact the PTA president and homeroom mothers.
15. Some of the children may be involved in city and church choirs, or music memory contests that require early submission of forms.
16. Plan any field trips obtain approval. Book buses for transportation.
17. Organize teaching materials based on the curriculum and developmentally appropriate practice. For example, make a song retrieval system with the song name, meter, pitches used, rhythm durations, form, and cross-references to other learning.
18. Make long-range plans. Organize a set of lesson plans for the first three months.

What to do the first day.   The first day is extremely important to set the tone of the class and begin the initial trust between child and adult.

1. Establish a favorable social climate. For example, use nametags and greeting songs to help the children feel comfortable. Consider playing a selection of music softly while the children enter (e.g., Sousa march).
2. Select a name game such as the *Name Chant.*
   ### Name Chant
   Start patting legs with steady beat and chant,
   "I can do this beat from my seat, I have a name and it sounds like this!"
   Teacher says name while patting legs and then says each child's name followed by the whole class saying that child's name in unison.
3. Assign each child, by name, their own spot (usually on the floor). Where the classroom teachers has nametags already made for the students, simply request that each child wears a nametag for the first few music lessons.
4. In the lesson include a wide range of short experiences; including simple game songs, moving, listening, playing instruments, and a story.
5. Plan for assessment in the lesson of the children's abilities for steady beat, singing, moving, listening, and playing classroom instruments.

6. Verbally tell the children the expectations, classroom rules, and consequences for unwanted behavior.
7. Have a lineup song or activity. For example, use clothing, colors or birthday months.

What to do the first week
1. Continue the diagnostic activities in the lessons (usually as games) to assess the children's music abilities.
2. Organize general plans and classroom procedures (opening activity is followed by prereading or music reading, movement, and so forth).
3. Reinforce learning by repetition of experiences.
4. Begin developing substitute lesson plans for each class that a musically untrained teacher can use. For example, a good quality video or a fun unskilled game such as "Music Bingo" is better than leaving the substitute with nothing to use.
5. Assign monitors or helpers in the older classes (K and above). The monitors are to be rotated each week.

What to do the first month
1. Base planning on the results of diagnostic assessment as well as curriculum. Consult the national standards and the school's curriculum.
2. Begin to plan for public appearances such as the holiday concerts and PTA programs.
3. Make two envelopes per class labeled yes and no. Place each child's name on an index card into the no envelope. As each child gets a special duty or activity to lead, place that child's name into the yes envelope so that everyone gets a turn..
4. The rest of the first year is based on what the children are able to do and decisions about curriculum.

Summary and Key Points

Good music instruction uses clear objectives that can be assessed and the results acted upon for the next steps in instruction. National, state, district, and school standards may be available for organizing teaching. Effective instruction arranges objectives in a sequence that lead to mastery. In a developmentally appropriate curriculum assessment is integrated into continuous observational assessment designed to improve the teaching—learning environment.

1. Plans for the first few class sessions need to be based on overall goals for the children and the assessment of what the child can do and understand today.
2. Keep in mind overall goals for the children. For example, what musical skills and concepts do you want them to possess when they leave school after four years, after one year, after one month, after one day?

3. The most important affective objective is the child's positive disposition toward music and music learning.
4. Make provision in plans for the uniqueness of the individual child. For example, plan child-centered experiences such as free and guided exploration of instruments.
5. Plan, plan, and over plan. It is difficult to plan too much!
6. Lesson plans are tangible evidence of instructional decisions. Design them carefully and thoughtfully.
7. Review summary lists from this chapter including national standards, taxonomy example, developmentally appropriate assessment, ways to manage, attention focusing techniques, and what to do before the first music class.

8
Experiences: Listening

Listening skill permeates all music activities. It is difficult to think of a musical activity that does not have a listening component. Listening includes various experiences ranging from identifying instrument color (e.g., trumpet versus a clarinet) to auditory discrimination task such as deciding if two phrases are the same or different.

Research

Chapter 4 provided a detailed view of music listening in infancy. This chapter examines listening for young children after the first year. More detailed information is contained in several general reviews (Flohr, 2001; Flohr and Hodges, 2002; Haack, 1992; Hedden, 1980, 1981; Lewis, 1989; Thompson and Schellenberg, 2002), a review for hearing disabilities (Darrow, 1989), and a review about music therapy for infants (Standley, 2002).

Melody and Harmony

Key and harmony. As indicated in Chapter 4, infants are able to detect out-of-key changes (Trainor and Trehub, 1992). Trainor and Trehub (1994) gave five- and seven-year-olds the listening task of hearing a half-step change, a whole-step change that went against the harmony but stayed in the key, and a two-step change that worked with the key and harmony. The five-year-olds found the half-step change easiest to detect, while the seven-year-olds found the whole-step change against the harmony was easier to detect than the two-step change. The researchers postulated that the seven-year-olds showed awareness of the key as well as the implied harmony. Krumhansl and Keil (1982) gave a stimulus to six- to eleven-year-old children that defined a key and then offered a single pitch. The children rated how each single pitch of the chromatic scale fit into the set key. Between the ages of six and eleven, the children's performance dramatically improved probably as a result of maturation and enculturation.

Intervals. Schellenberg and Trehub (1996a) found that both adults and six-year-old children were able to detect changes in interval of a half step (e.g., on the piano moving from middle C to the black key C sharp directly above). But the success was limited to perfect intervals (C and C an octave higher, C and F or C and G played simultaneously).

Table 8.1 Selected Listening Research (also see Table 3.2 and Chapter 4 for infant studies)

AUTHOR	AGE	N	SUMMARY OF SELECTED FINDINGS
Sims (1986)	3–5	96	Wide variation in children's total listening time. Individual children were very consistent in the time spent listening to each of four selections. Active listening resulted in higher (or similar) attention to the music than passive activities. No difference in amount of time spent listening to familiar versus unfamiliar classical music.
Bella, et al. (2001)	3–8 & adult	67 / 24	Task was to decide if classical Western music excerpts were happy or sad. 3–4s did not distinguish emotion. 5s were affected by tempo change and 6–8s affected by mode and tempo.
Godeli, et al. (1996)	Preschool	27	During and after listening to music social behaviors increased. Type of music was not significant.
Malyarenko, et al. (1996)	4	43	Found that an exposure to music of one hour per day over a six-month period was found to have an effect on the brain's electrical activity.
Peery & Peery (1986)	4 yrs. 7 mon.	45	Children exposed to classical selection over 10 months preferred the classical music. Pretest/posttest design yielded no significant changes for the control group.
Sims (2001)	4 yrs. 8 mon.	18	Children demonstrated consistent listening patterns of wide variation but consistent individual patterns as in Sims (1986). Research was in naturalistic setting of music centers with free choice for listening.
Abel-Struth (1981)	5–7	42	Children able to evaluate music in terms of (in order of preference) marchlike, signallike, dancelike, songlike, animal sound, and flowing sound.
Moore & Staum (1987)	5–7	180	Short-term memory for auditory skill. 5s did well with 3–4 tone patterns accompanied by color images (from the game 'Simon'). 7s mastered five tone patterns.
Flohr & Miller (1995)	5–7	13	Longitudinal study. EEG brain activity was different for two styles of music (Vivaldi & Irish folk song) for children at 7 years that was not different for the same children at five years.
Sims & Nolker (2002)	6 yrs. 1 mon.	48	Wide variation in total listening times, but individuals consistent in their own approach (time spent) in listening as in Sims (1986). No relationships of listening time and age or teacher ratings of attention.
Mills (1985)	6–16	1715	Analyzed responses to a pitch and rhythm (pulse) test. The responses were age related with most increases occurring up to age 10 or 11.
Hedden (1980; 1981)	Review	Review	Organized studies into three categories. Notated themes/visual representations with instruction not very effective in elementary grades. Composition experiences and live concert attendance enhanced various listening skills.
Haack (1992)	Review	Review	Review of research on listening responses to music, listening memory, imagery, and musical elements.
Hetland (2000)	Review	Review	Meta-analysis of listening studies show some positive effect but does not lead to a conclusion that exposing children to classical music will raise intelligence, academic achievement, or long-term spatial skills.
Thompson & Schellenberg (2002)	Review	Review	Review of research on pitch perception and cognition, melody, scales, harmony, rhythm, and timbre.

Rhythm and Issues of Interaction

Musicians normally think of music elements such as rhythm, melody, pitch, and intervals as independent and divisible parts of music. For young learners a generalization might be that depending on conditions of the task at hand, musical elements may interact with each other. For example, experienced teachers often note that young children find confusion in the process of learning the concept of high–low. As a child listens for high and low pitches several elements interact. Those elements may include pitch, loudness (loud has more energy and can be thought of as higher), spatial orientation (e.g., if a child is familiar with the piano, high on piano is to the right and low is to the left), and rhythm (e.g., a child may confuse fast music with music that is higher because fast music may be heard as having more energy than slow music).

Preferences

Young children are able to demonstrate preference for musical examples styles such as marchlike more than flowing sounds (Abel-Struth, 1981). Peery and Peery (1986) found that preschool children's preference for classical music as opposed to popular music was influenced by a ten-month exposure. Even day-old infants make choices about what music they wish to hear. One team of researchers gave neonates the choice of listening to excerpts of classical and rock music (Flohr, Atkins, Bower, and Aldridge, 2000). The neonates were able to manipulate which sound they heard by the use of a non-nutritive sucking device and demonstrated preference for one type of music. Most of the thirty-four neonates chose the classical excerpt (see also Chapter 3, prenatal).

Age-related Differences

Richardson (1996) found children with music training responded to many styles and genres of music with statements that were similar to adult musicians. Several studies in Table 8.1 found age-related differences. Two age spans are of particular interest. First, Mills (1989) reported most increases on a pitch and rhythm test occurred before age ten or eleven. Mill's findings support Gordon's idea of developmental music aptitude stabilizing around the age of eight or nine after which scores on music aptitude tests do not change to an appreciable degree (Chapter 3). Second, the five- to seven-year-old range correlates with Piaget's stage theories and findings in other fields (Janowsky and Carper, 1996).

Effects of Music Listening

Several researchers have examined the influence of background music on a number of variables including reading, motor performance, spatial abilities, beliefs and values, stress, social behaviors, consumer behavior such as increased purchase, and health care (Godeli, Santana, Souza, and Marquetti, 1996; Hetland, 2000; North, Hargreaves, and Tarrant, 2002; Radocy and Boyle, 1979).

Listening can be passive or active. Passive listening refers to listening during which the child is not overtly engaged with the music, for example, background music while the child is resting. Although labeled passive listening, it is clear from Chapter 4 that infants are aware and react to music. Active listening refers to listening during which the child is overtly engaged in listening. It is often difficult to tell with certainty if a child is actively listening but usually determined by the child's movements or expression. Examples include a two-year-old listening and moving to the rhythm or smiling at the point where the music changes tempo. A problem in research about young children's listening is that it is difficult to determine with certainty that a young child is actually listening to the music. A researcher can only devise ways to infer that the child is listening such as head-turn (Chapter 4) and use various methods of observation including measuring time spent with headphones and on-task behavior.

Task performance.   The inconsistent pattern of results in the literature are attributable to interactions among many factors (Chabris et al., 1999; Flohr and Hodges, 2002; Gruhn and Rauscher, 2002). Factors investigated include individual learners, type or nature of task (e.g., verbal, rhythmic), the way in which the task is measured (e.g., psychological test, ranking, type of brain imaging), research design, task difficulty, age of children, children's attention to the music, and children's motivations. There are, however, advances in neuroscience and developmental research that support the idea that music listening has a positive influence on young children (Flohr, 2001). For example, Malyrenko and colleagues found that an exposure to classical music of one hour per day over a six-month period had an effect on the brain's electrical activity in four-year-old children (Table 8.1). Brain activity measurement indicated that listening to music resulted in an enhancement of coherence (coherence reflects the number and strength of coordination between different brain locations). Some authors believe that coherence demonstrates evidence of anatomical connections and information exchange between two brain locations (Fein, Raz, and Merrin, 1988). Results from Sims' research (1986) (Table 8.1) and the opinion of a group of early childhood music educators (Flohr, 2001) indicate that active listening will produce more attentive listening than passive listening alone.

Social behaviors.   In a study of preschoolers, social interactions increased after music listening (Godeli et al., 1996). Gender and type of music did not make a difference (children's choirs singing folk music with instrument accompaniment and heavy rock by Deff-Leopard).

Health concerns.   Infant studies have shown several positive effects from music listening including less time in the isolette, less total time in intensive care, less weight loss, more nonstress behaviors, fewer high-arousal states, and positive effects on oxygen saturation levels, heart rate, and respiration (Standley, 2002). Also, Darrow (1989) reviewed thirty-six studies about music and the hearing impaired. Her suggestions for working with hearing impaired children included using louder dynamic levels, using instruments of sustained tone (e.g., electronic keyboard) to provide more useful feedback to the hearing impaired than short duration percussion instruments (e.g., woodblock), and hearing impaired children are often more responsive to the rhythm than to the tonal aspects of music.

Developmental Milestones

Table 8.2 lists milestones set to approximate ages. Individual children exhibit large listening skill differences; their skills generally improve with age, experience, and instruction.

Table 8.2   Milestones in Listening

MONTHS	MILESTONE
0–3	Turns head toward a musical sound. Expresses satisfaction or distress with different kinds of vocal sounds. Quiets to music (not all music, e.g., most probably will quiet to music heard in utero). Responds to sharp sounds (e.g., click of light switch).
0–12	Infants are surprisingly proficient music listeners. Infants demonstrate a preference for consonant as opposed to dissonant intervals (e.g. P4 or C-F over A4 or C-F#). They are even able to detect a mistuned tone in ascending-descending scales of various types. They are more attentive to intact musical phrases than phrases disrupted by brief silent intervals of time. The infant may detect out-of-key or harmony changes better than adults. Infants prefer positive emotional tone. They also show more interest in singing than in speech. Maternal singing reduces infant arousal more than maternal speech (Ch. 4).
6–8	Searches for sound with eyes. Cries on hearing intense sounds or when music is withdrawn.
9–14	Orients to spoken or sung name. Reacts to novel features of musical instruments.
12–24	Attends to music for several minutes.
24	Play music at various tempi including those of 120–200 bpm and the child's natural response is to move or dance to the music.
36	Begin listening to tonal and rhythm patterns. Child is ready to sing and/or play short 2–4 sound patterns and can engage in games with step-bells and other melodic instruments (see Experiences).
36–72	Child is acquiring many words. This age range is an optimum time for language development and musical development. For example, a child hearing a language during this age period will retain native speaker accent. In the same way, a child hearing music during this age period will retain many nuances of musical sound.
60	Able to distinguish happy and sad emotions affected by tempo (Table 8.1, Bella).
60–84	Able to identify instruments such as drum, trumpet, flute, clarinet, and violin as belonging to families of instruments (strings, woodwind, brass, percussion). Several studies find a change or **shift** in listening (Ch. 3 & Table 8.1, Bella, Flohr, & Moore).
55	Exposure to a music style may increase preference for that style (Table 8.1).
72	Able to detect half-step consonant interval changes. 6 to 8-year-olds affected by mode and tempo when listening for emotion in music (Table 8.1, Bella).

Steps to Successful Listening Experiences
Pitfalls to Avoid

Avoid loud music to prevent possible hearing damage. Use repeated listening of the same piece and guided listening so that the children become familiar with the music. The term guided listening refers to listening lessons guided by the teacher with an objective in mind (e.g., examples of experiences, No. 8). Repeated and guided listening is needed if the objective is to show musical qualities such as melodic contour, tone color, and instruments. For example, if a string quartet is to play in the elementary school, the music teacher should prepare the children by repeated listening to the pieces to be performed so that the children are familiar with the music.

Selection of Music

- Provide a wide variety of styles. Include music from different periods, cultures, tempi, styles, and with harmonic diversity, instruments including vocal music, and examples of tonalities (minor, major, modal, non-Western). Listen to music that is complex and challenging as well as music developed for children. Young children respond positively to many styles of music because they have not yet developed strong preferences based on musical style characteristics (Sims, 1987; Sims and Cassidy, 1997). Give children a chance to hear styles of music that they normally do not hear. The optimum time to introduce many styles of music to children is in the early years (Flohr, 2001; Peery and Peery, 1986; Sims, 2002).
- Begin with selections that have clear and easily identifiable characteristics. Younger children have difficulty centering their listening on more than one element at a time. As experience is gained, (after age five), children enjoy music with contrasting sections (see experience No. 8).

Teacher Behaviors

The way in which a teacher presents music for listening is likely to affect the children's attention and attitudes (Peery and Peery, 1986; Sims, 2002).

- Preschool children's attention is likely to be improved by high levels of teacher eye contact and by engaging the children in hand movement activities directly related to the music (Sims, 1986).
- Be sure to model good listening behavior by not talking while the music is playing. If the purpose is to point out a significant change in the music (e.g., when a new instrument enters), stop the music to talk about the change or use a prop, picture, or puppet to nonverbally indicate the change.

Strategies

- Use both group and free individual choice listening formats. When children are free to choose, there is a wide variety in how long they listen. However, each individual child is consistent in the amount of time spent listening to each selection (Table 8.1). During beginning group listening the selections need to be shorter durations of one to three minutes. In addition to group listening, children should have access to a listening area (especially for children who enjoy listening for longer periods of time).
- Use props such as scarves, puppets, and pictures of instruments and animals that are related to the music. For example, if listening to *Peter and the Wolf,* use pictures or puppets to represent instruments and animal characters (Prokofiev, Saint-Saëns, and Britten, n.d.).
- Provide live performers from the school and community. Bring individuals or the class to live concerts. Use real instruments for the children's exploration.
- Use the most advanced and high quality sound equipment possible.
- Children can respond to and understand music terminology and concepts better than they can use the terminology themselves (Costa-Giomi and Descombes, 1996).
- Repeated listening helps the music become familiar and reinforces learning such as identification of the sound of a trumpet or violin.
- Drawing a picture while listening to music is **not** a music listening experience. If the objective is to integrate music and drawing, try asking the children to draw the contour of a melody.

Examples of Listening Experiences

In the examples below, numerous other sources for listening experiences are available (Choksy et al., 2001; Feierabend, 2000a, 2000b, 2000c; Flohr, 2001; Sims, 1995).

1. *Infant and parent/caregiver (Steady beat and listening: birth-infancy).* Play, sing, or chant music and walk your fingers up and down the baby's arm to the steady beat while listening to music (see Feierabend's books, Chapter 6, for similar ideas).
2. *Toddler and parent/caregiver (Playing and listening; one to three years).* Encourage the child to make music while listening to a recording. Offer the child a small child-safe instrument such as egg maracas, small maracas, or another instrument that fits the style of the music. Model playing an instrument to the beat of the music—children like to imitate adults.
3. *Instrument game (Listening, discriminating; three years and above).* Choose two instruments that have very distinct sound qualities, for

example, maracas and woodblock. Demonstrate the sound of each and, if possible, make the instruments available in a music center for use by all the children. Go behind a screen or other visual blocking device and play one instrument. The game is to decide which instrument was played. Extend and challenge the children by adding instruments and by making the instruments very similar in sound (e.g., egg maracas and large maracas). Three-year-olds will find it difficult to discriminate between small maracas with a handle and small egg maracas. As the children are able to discriminate between two instruments, change the instruments and later use three and four instruments.

4. *Identify the song rhythm (Identify rhythm patterns; three years and above)*. Begin with two known songs such as, *Twinkle, Twinkle* and *If You're Happy and You Know It*. Ask, "Which song's (*Twinkle* or *If You're*) words sound like this rhythm" and clap the rhythm of one of the songs. After the child makes a choice, sing the song while clapping the rhythm to see if the rhythm and song match. Demonstrate how the correct answer matches the rhythm. Choice of songs, song length, complexity of rhythm, and the children's familiarity with the songs will determine the difficulty. For three- to four-year-olds use two choices and very familiar songs. For older children, use three or four songs and occasionally include a song that is not well known. A more difficult task for young children is to determine if two rhythm patterns (not necessarily from known songs) are same of different.

5. *Melody with Montessori bells (Listening for melodic movement; five years and above)*. The mushroom bells come as a set of eight white and a set of eight black bells. Line the two sets so that they are arranged from high to low and the parent/teacher and the child (or two children) sit side to side. Play a short melodic pattern beginning with just two pitches. The child's task is to repeat the pattern (they will have a visual clue of how the parent/teacher moves the mallet from bell to bell, but all the bells look alike). As the child succeeds, gradually increase the number of pitches to imitate.

6. *Tonal patterns (Listening for patterns; three years and older)*. Many methods in Chapter 6 such as those by Gordon and Kodály emphasize learning tonal patterns. For example, the pattern sol-mi-do is common to many songs such as *Dixie, The National Anthem, Roll Over* (Smith and Leonhard, 1968), and the *Sesame Street Song*. Model playing the pitches C–A–F on a step bell (a series of eight bells arranged from low to high on a small wooden staircase). Ask the children to play the pattern when it occurs in the song while singing.

7. *Peter and the Wolf (Listening and instruments; three years and above)*. Sergey Prokofiev set this classic children's tale to music for narrator and orchestra. His composition is an example of *program* music. Several instruments are used to signify characters in the story (e.g., oboe

for the duck) and the music helps children learn about the timbre (tone color) of orchestral instruments. A Sony CD also includes the *Carnival of the Animals*, a zoological fantasy by Saint-Saëns and Britten's *Young Person's Guide to the Orchestra* (Prokofiev et al.).

8. *Guitar and piano (Listening and identifying sounds of instruments; five years and above).* Manuel Ponce's *Guitar Sonata*, second movement, provides another opportunity to learn about timbre (Ponce, 1999). The movement begins with the piano playing a phrase containing three notes that mimics *Twinkle, Twinkle, Little Star.* The solo guitar repeats the phrase. Use pictures of a piano and a guitar.

9. *Expand ideas of listening (Listening; three years and above).* Try some of the following ideas: sound exploration around the room, create a sound exploration center, explore body sounds, imitate sounds (e.g., birds), classify and compare sounds found in explorations (louder-softer, higher-lower, faster-slower, same and different rhythms and tonal patterns), select sound effects and music for stories, and respond to sound with movement.

Summary and Key Points

Listening permeates all music activities. Whenever children engage in music experiences, they also engage in listening. Key points are:

1. Children are able to hear sounds including music while in the womb.
2. Sing to infants and young children.
3. Provide music of the highest possible quality especially music performed expressively.
4. If possible, play an instrument for the child or class.
5. Involve children as active participants.
6. Listen, analyze, describe, and classify sounds from nature and man-made music sounds.
7. Provide music of different tempi—slower and faster examples. For naptime use music slower than 100 bpm.
8. Sounds before signs; give the children much experience in listening (and singing, creating, moving) before reading and writing (the Pestalozzian adage) (Hair, 1982).

9

Experiences:
Singing

Joanne Rutkowski and Valerie L. Trollinger

Introduction

This chapter is the longest chapter in the section on experiences, because research and knowledge from both voice science and music education are discussed. The chapter begins with an investigation of the nature of the very young voice then applies that information to nurturing the voices of young children. Children with healthy voices, and the neurobiological ability to process musical pitch (Ayotte, Peretz, and Hyde, 2002), are capable of learning to sing and many do so at an early age. Singing is a complex muscular activity; the reader is advised to review the vocal health section of this chapter to aid the development of healthy singing.

Most children seem to be natural musicians and singers, but by the time some children enter kindergarten they seem reluctant to sing and have difficulty singing successfully. Without help and encouragement from singing teachers and parents, these children may never sing freely and their lives will be void of this natural form of music experience.

Background

It is important that the reader have an understanding of the physiological nature of the vocal mechanism. With an understanding of how the vocal mechanism grows and develops from birth to age six years, one may better understand how children's voices are different from adult voices and how to work with them. For more information readers are encouraged to refer to books such as Kenneth Phillips's *Teaching Kids to Sing* (1992), Oren Brown's *Discover Your Voice* (1996), and the five-volume work *Excellence in Singing* by Joan Wall and R. Caldwell (2001). The following system for pitch is used throughout this chapter:

C4 = Middle C (The middle note on the piano. D4 the D above middle C).
C3 = the C one octave below middle C.
C5 = the C one octave above middle C.

The Vocal Mechanism in Adults and Children

The voice is not only the first musical **instrument** a child possesses, but also the only one that is played as it develops, from birth until death, inside the body. The way the voice works is difficult to grasp because it is within the human body. Using the analogy of singing as a kind of vocal ballet may prove helpful. Both ballet and singing are (1) psychomotor skills; (2) require precision movements; (3) use cartilages, muscles, and ligaments, (4) aim for gracefulness in movement, not jerkiness; (5) make simultaneous use of vertical, lateral, and rocking movements; and (6) if not executed properly, may result in physical injury. As ballet is an athletic event for the body, singing is an athletic event for the vocal mechanism. A ballet teacher needs to have a basic awareness of what the body can do physically for effective teaching and learning, and to prevent painful accidents. Likewise, someone who is going to be involved in teaching singing, even at a very basic level, should have an understanding of the physical workings of the voice.

Basic vocal sounds for both speech and singing are produced by way of the interactive functions of the **respiratory system**, and the **larynx**. In this chapter, only the larynx is discussed in some anatomical detail, as it is assumed that the reader is familiar with the anatomy of the respiratory system. The distance from the larynx to the mouth is referred to as the **vocal tract**, and shortening or lengthening the tract will aid in creating high and low sounds. Also included in the vocal tract are the **resonators**—the mouth, sinuses, and throat.

The larynx serves multiple purposes (Brown, 1996) and is composed of very small muscles, cartilages, and ligaments (Figure 9.1). Because the larynx is not attached to the skeleton, it is able to move up and down, which will shorten or lengthen the vocal tract (similar to a slide whistle action). Observe this happen by watching a grown man as he speaks, sings, or swallows: in a man, the thyroid cartilage tips forward, creating the Adam's apple. As he speaks, the Adam's apple will move up and down in a kind of front-to-back rocking motion. Lengthening and shortening the vocal tract will help create lower and higher sounds in the voice.

The inside of the larynx is where the crucial task of sound production (phonation) takes place when delicate muscular tissues known as the vocal bands (also referred to as vocal cords) are set into motion. When the bands are subjected to air pressure generated by the lungs, they will start to vibrate. The bands can vibrate in many ways, depending upon the size of the opening between the bands (to let the air through), how long and stiff they are at the time, and the degree of power of the sound. Although many internal mechanisms contribute to how wide the bands are opened and how long and stiff they are, two particular muscle pairs are primarily responsible for these kinds of movement: the *thyroarytenoids (TA)* control the amount of opening between the vocal bands, and the *cricothyroids (CT)* control how long and stiff they become. For example, the more the bands lengthen and stiffen, the stronger the breath pressure, the higher the sound; the less the bands lengthen and stiffen, the lesser the breath pressure, the lower the sound. In addition, the physical length of

Side   **Above**

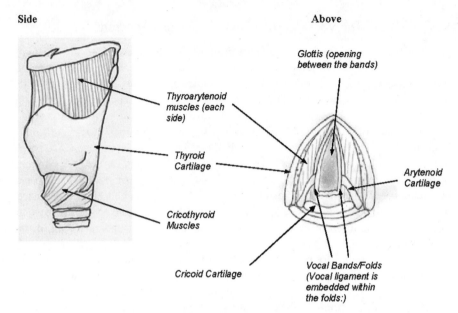

Figure 9.1   The external and internal cross-section of the larynx
viewed from side and above (simplified).
Illustrated by V. L. Trollinger

the vocal bands affects the pitch of the sound: longer bands will generate lower
sounds and shorter bands will generate higher sounds. In adult females, the bands can
be 11–17 mm in length, and for men, they can be 15–21 mm in length. The presence
of longer bands is the primary reason why men have lower voices than women. The
bands are attached in a parallel fashion to the **vocal ligament**, which is often referred
to as the true vocal cord structure. The vocal ligament attaches the thyroarytenoids to
the cricothyroids, which allows for wider ranges of high sounds and low sounds.

All of the muscles inside the larynx, along with many others directly outside of it,
are attached to particular cartilages and ligaments so the entire mechanism can move
in many different ways. In the adult, the cartilages ossify (become bones), giving the
vocal mechanism more stability and control over the sounds it produces, but also
requiring more muscular strength to make the mechanism work. If these muscles are
not exercised, they will lose the ability to function properly. If exercised regularly,
the result is a wide singing range with much control and agility that can last a life-
time.

The cartilages, ligaments, and muscles controlling the vocal bands and laryngeal
movement need to interact with each other in a balanced manner (see Vocal regis-
ters/adjustment) for healthy singing and speech to occur. An untrained singer may
inadvertently work these mechanisms in a very unbalanced manner, by forcing one
mechanism to work in resistance to the others.

After speech or singing sounds have been generated via the interaction of the larynx and respiratory system, they are subject to the degree of **resonance** that is influenced by the throat, sinuses, and mouth cavities. For example, a voice that has a lot of resonance is that of the actor James Earl Jones, who provided the voice of Darth Vader in the original *Star Wars* movies. When one sings or speaks, the majority of the sounds produced move out of the mouth and into the resonating areas in sound energy waves.

The Child's Vocal Mechanism

The child larynx differs greatly from the adult larynx, discussed above, and does not function the same way in singing. At birth, the infant larynx more closely resembles that of a nonhuman primate (Bosma, 1975; Kent, 1981). Over the first six months of life the larynx undergoes dramatic change, along with the rest of the vocal tract, to more closely resemble the adult version (Sasaki, Suzuki, and Horiuchi, 1977). The primary function of the infant larynx is to protect the airway and to aid in swallowing. Therefore, it is placed particularly high in the vocal tract to keep the child from choking while eating. The high placement of the larynx in the vocal tract results in the infant vocalizing in a fairly high range. After the first six months of life, the larynx begins a gradual descent, less dramatic for girls than for boys, that continues through life.

In addition to the high position of the larynx in the vocal tract, there are several other physiological differences from the adult larynx. Until the age of two to three years the vocal bands of the larynx are composed of mostly mucosal (like mucous) rather than fibrous (like fibers in muscle) tissue (Titze, 1992), and the vocal ligament is not yet present (Andrews and Summers, 2001; Sataloff, Spiegel, and Rosen, 1998). These bands are also very short (6–8 mm in infancy) (Sataloff, 1997). Because of the absence of the vocal ligament and the presence of mucosal vocal bands, the young child may have difficulty controlling voice sounds. At birth, the cricothyroid muscle pair (CT) is the largest muscle in the larynx, but the thyroarytenoid muscle pair (TA) is essentially an undefined mass of tissue (Sataloff et al., 1998). However, as the thyroarytenoids (which control degrees of opening and closing of the vocal bands) begin to take shape around the age of two, the child begins to gain some consistent control over the range of pitches made. The mucosal vocal bands the child possesses at birth are not the true vocal cord structure that will begin to develop between the ages of one and four years (Andrews and Summers, 2001; Sataloff et al., 1998). As the vocal ligament is not present, many of the high and low sounds infants and very young children make are primarily due to the raising and lowering of the larynx, which lengthens and shortens the vocal tract, and results in a limited number of controlled sounds that could be used for vocalizing. The vocal ligament remains weak until the age of six years, and at that point it starts to become layered and fibrous, adding more vocal stability and control. This layering process continues until approximately the age of sixteen years (Morrison and Rammage, 1994). The degree of development of the vocal ligament in relationship to the growth of surrounding muscles and cartilage structures may directly affect the development of singing registers and singing range. At present, there is no research available that directly addresses this relationship in children's singing development, although physiologically a connection seems logical as the vocal ligament is what allows humans to develop a wider singing range by providing the ability to create higher pitches (Titze, 1996). The vocal ligament, laryngeal musculature, and cartilages are all underdeveloped in the infant; through early childhood these begin to develop and take shape, but they do not function together as an adult singing voice until the late teen years. The progression of physical vocal development in relation to speech and singing development is presented in Table 9.1.

Another area of interest in relation to the infant and preschool voice is the development of the respiratory system. Even though infants have smaller vocal tracts and shorter vocal bands, which means their sounds will be higher, they can make these higher sounds at a very strong amplitude (very loud dynamic) because the infant respiratory system is smaller than the adult system. Research suggests that infants work 50–60 percent harder with their lungs than adults do to make these louder sounds (Stathopoulos and Sapienza, 1991). Because of the underdeveloped respiratory system, young children have to take many breaths when they talk and sing.

The interaction of the child larynx and respiratory system allows for the production of sound that may be less resonant than that of an adult in speech or singing. With maturity and proper development of healthy vocal behaviors, healthy resonance can be developed, which will affect the way the child uses the voice to sing. But it is not a good idea to push this concept too soon. Titze (1992) and Miller (2000) have cautioned that having young children sing songs in adult ranges and of adult length will do a disservice to their developing respiratory and vocal systems.

Research and Theories Concerned with the Young Voice in Speech and Singing

This section addresses the research and resulting theories of how children learn to speak and sing, how they use vocal registration in singing, and how they learn songs. Issues that the research and theories generate follow the discussion. Although the research in anatomy and speech has presented consistent findings about development, the research concerned with singing development has provided less consistent findings.

Speaking Voice Development

Very young children often exhibit babbling behavior, which is primarily seen as a precursor to language development (Blake and Fink, 1987; Eilers and Oller, 1988; Moog, 1976a; Vihman and Miller, 1988). Although it is generally believed that infant babble sounds are similar across cultural and linguistic boundaries until the age of

Table 9.1 Vocal Development Milestones for Birth–6 Years

AGE	PHYSIOLOGICAL CHARACTERISTICS	VOCALIZATION/SPEECH CHARACTERISTICS	SINGING DEVELOPMENT
0–4 months	Larynx situated very high in the vocal tract. Cricothyroid (CT) is largest muscle in larynx. Thyroarytenoid muscle not developed. No vocal ligament. Tissues are mucosal rather than fibrous. Vocal fold length approximates 6–8 mm in infant.	Birth cry is @ 500 Hz (C above middle C) (Sataloff, 1998). Has different cries or vocalizations for specific discomforts (2 months) (Stillman, 1978)	
4–12 months	Larynx begins slow drop. Respiratory system still underdeveloped (continues to grow and strengthen throughout childhood).	Vocalizes to get attention (Stillman, 1978). May exhibit a wide pitch range. (G3 to C6 found when measuring spontaneous vocalizations.) Imitates vocalizations of the teacher/adult with prompting (9 months) (Stillman, 1978).	
12–18 months	Very thin and nonlayered vocal ligament begins to appear (from ages 1–4 years).	Vocally imitates others without prompting (Eilers & Oller, 1988; Stillman, 1978). Voice fundamental frequency @ 340–470 Hz (E4–A4) (Titze, 1992; Wilson, 1987). Wide vocalization range may still be evident. Vocal sounds may be closely identified to native language to be learned (de Boysson-Bardies, Halle, Sagart, & Durand, 1989; Kuehn, 1985).	Plays with vocal sounds (Davidson, McKernon, & Gardner, 1981; McDonald & Simons, 1989).
19 months			Melodic and rhythmic patterns begin to appear in vocalizations (Davidson et al., 1981; McDonald & Simons, 1989).
19–24 months		Development of 1–2 word phrases, uses voice to impart emotional meaning (e.g., NO said very loudly), develops a jargon, such as "wah" for water, "bah-bah" for blanket (Stillman, 1978). Wide vocalization range may still be evident (not in singing).	Creates short, spontaneous songs with small melodic intervals and flexible rhythm patterns. Range used for vocalizing with intent to sing is quite small. Able to learn to produce short repating melodic patterns from simple songs closer to 24 months (Davidson et al., 1981; McDonald & Simons, 1989).

Table 9.1 Continued

AGE	PHYSIOLOGICAL CHARACTERISTICS	VOCALIZATION/SPEECH CHARACTERISTICS	SINGING DEVELOPMENT
24 months	TA begins to take shape. Ossification of some cartilages begins (continues until age 65 years).	Vocalization range may begin to narrow, or may continue to widen depending upon reinforcement of vocalization skill. (Sinor, 1984; Trollinger, 2001; Wendrich, 1981). Language acquisition begins (may affect voice usage). Voice Fo average is 340–470 Hz. (E4 to A4) (Wilson, 1987).	Use of melodic patterns or bits from learned songs into spontaneous singing. May start to confuse loudness with pitch (e.g., to sing higher, will instead vocalize louder) (Titze, 1992).
2–3 years	Vocal ligament still very weak. Thyroarytenoid developing.	By age 3, child can state his or her first and last name, gender, and recent happenings: can express physical and emotional states, and imitate the voices of characters in stories. Voice fundamental frequency average is @ 255–360 Hz (C4–F#4) (Titze, 1992; Wilson, 1987).	Imitates short songs or melodies, but not always accurately. May change melody to better accommodate his/her voice range.
4 years	Continued weak vocal ligament and continued thyroarytenoid development.	Speaks in complete sentences (Stillman, 1978). Voice frequency is @ B3 to F#4 (240–340 Hz) (Titze, 1992; Wilson, 1987). Vocalization depends on individual development and learned vocal habits (Sataloff, 1997).	Learning songs generally follows this sequence: words, rhythm, phrases, and melodic shape (Davidson et al., 1981; McDonald & Simons, 1989). Possible beginnings of vocal singing registration emerge (due to thyroarytenoid development and vocal ligament development): however, may be very individualistic. Research directly addressing this relationship is not yet available.
5–6 years	At 6, vocal ligament starts to become layered and fibrous, which leads to more vocal stability and control. This process continues until the late teen years.	Voice fundamental frequency generally @225–325 Hz (A3–D4) or so (Titze, 1992; Wilson, 1987). Again, highly variable. Physiologic vocal range is fairly stable (remains through childhood) (Sataloff, 1997).	Sense of key is stabilized, can sing fairly accurately (Davidson et al., 1981; McDonald & Simons, 1989). Increased singing range can develop (Sataloff, 1997) if voice is healthy. Musical range may increase due to vocal ligament development and other maturation factors.

Note: The tables in this chapter use the following system. C4=Middle C; D4=D above Middle C; E4=E above Middle C; F4=F above Middle C; F#4=F# above Middle C; B3=B below Middle C; A3=A below Middle C. Fo=Fundamental Frequency.

one year (Kuehn, 1985), some researchers have found that babble differs between these boundaries (de Boysson-Bardies, Halle, Sagart, and Durand, 1989).

Children who have moved beyond babbling and are verbal (around the age of two years) have been studied to determine mean speech frequency and the overall speech frequency range. As Table 9.1 shows, there is a lot of variability in the pitch level of children's speech voices depending upon how they were assessed and how their voices matured. For an excellent summary of research concerned with children's voice frequencies, see Wilson (1987). Children often imitate the speech patterns of parents and other important adults, and it is by doing so that they learn to add intonations that may be perceived as having emotional context and meaning. However, in languages other than English such as Cantonese and Mandarin, the pitch of the word also imparts the linguistic meaning. For example, "ma" in these languages can mean either mother, horse, flax, or serve as an expression of anger, depending on where it is pitched tonally by the voice (DeMente, 1995; Hu and Lee, 1992). How a child uses his or her voice is highly individualized, and is strongly influenced by the native culture in which s/he lives and familial vocal use.

Speech and singing research has, until recently, been conducted separately, with little attention paid to how one may directly affect the other. New research in this area undertaken by a number of researchers (Chen-Hafteck, 1998; Rutkowski and Chen-Hafteck, 2001; Rutkowski, Chen-Hafteck, and Gluschankof, 2002; Trollinger, 2001, 2003) has indicated that the native language and personal speech characteristics of a child may affect the manner in which the child consequently uses his/her voice to sing. These findings have given support to Gould's (1968) assertion that the speech voice cannot be ignored when addressing singing skill development: often, poor speech habits will translate to poor singing habits, and good speech habits could aid the development of singing to some degree.

Singing Voice Development

Discrepancies in research findings may be due to the different ways in which the children's voices have been assessed for pitch or may reflect the great variance in young children's singing behaviors. In studying infant and preverbal children's voices, all vocal sounds, including pitched sounds that likely would not contribute to the acquisition of singing, have been included. This may give an inflated view of range. A summary of observed vocal ranges of young children is presented in Table 9.2. The ranges observed in varying situations may not reflect the ranges children would exhibit in nurturing musical environments. For specific voice ranges found by each researcher and details regarding each study, refer to the source indicated in Table 9.2.

Researchers have also investigated the pitch that children select when they start singing a song on their own. Four- to six-year-olds begin songs on C4 or D4 (Kirkpatrick, 1962; Plumridge, 1972; Porter, 1977; Thurloway, 1977; Wilson, 1973). However, Kostka (1984) found that the midpoint of four- to five-year-olds' singing

Table 9.2   Observed Singing Ranges of Children

AGES	RANGES	RESEARCH SOURCES
3–9 months	G3 to C6	Fox (1990), Michel (1973)
7 months to 3 years	A3 to G5	Ries (1987), Simons (1964)
2 years	D4 to A4	Jersild & Bienstock (1934)
	A3-flat to C5	Alford (1971)
	Lowest A3-flat	Michel (1973)
	C4 to C5	McKernon (1979)
3 years	C4 to A4 or B4	Jersild & Bienstock (1931)
	G3 to C5	Alford (1971), Updegraff, Heliger & Learned (1938)
	B3-flat - G4-flat	Harkey (1978/1979)
4 years	B3 to C5	Jersild & Bienstock (1934)
	A3-flat to C5	Alford (1971)
5 years	A3 to D5	Jersild & Bienstock (1934)
	B3 to G4	Updegraff, Heliger & Learned (1938)
	A3 to B4	Cleall (1970)
	B3-flat–G4-flat	Joyner (1971)
	C4 to A4	Plumridge (1972)
	B3-flat–G4-flat	Young (1971)

appears to be around E4-flat. These pitches are within the mean speech frequency ranges of young children, perhaps indicating young children's lack of distinction between their speaking and singing voices, either cognitively, physically, or a combination of both. The difference in reported research begs for further inquiry using current technology.

Vocal Registers/Vocal Adjustment

The terms vocal registers, registration events, shifts, and breaks are often used in singing. These words are attempts to give a name to what is thought to be physically happening inside the larynx when the quality of tone in a voice changes. Sundberg (1987) provides an analogy that the shifting of the voice is not unlike—at least perceptually—the shifting of a gear mechanism in a car. In a car, using an inappropriate gear at a certain speed is inefficient and may even damage the engine. Similarly, using an inappropriate register to sing at a certain pitch level, over time will damage the vocal mechanism.

The term **register** in voice science refers to phenomena in which the sounds are produced using similar adjustments of the vocal mechanism and breath. For example, growling like a dog and then meowing like a newborn kitten requires one to use two different adjustments or registers. These kinds of registers are common in all human voices, but are not generally used for singing, nor will they contribute to the development of singing skills. However, one register, the **modal adjustment,** which is used for both speech and singing, is important for our purposes.

Singers often use the terms **head** voice and **chest** voice, both part of the modal adjustment, to describe the physical sensations of sound produced while singing. Both of these outmoded terms have been replaced by the more appropriate **lighter adjustment** for the head voice and **heavy adjustment** for the chest voice. Both adjustments, plus their mixtures, are used in healthy singing. Briefly and generally stated, these terms refer to degrees of antagonistic muscular tension between the cricothyroids and thyroarytenoids as mediated by the vocal ligament. The motion created by this force is of an internal lateral rocking nature, due to the lengthening and stiffening of the vocal bands.

Young children make their pitched vocalizations for speech and singing by moving the larynx up and down, thus creating a shorter or longer pharynx, not unlike a slide whistle. It is not until the development of a functioning vocal ligament that the registration events specific to singing can happen. Anatomical dissections (e.g., Kahane, 1975) and more recently electron microscope studies (e.g., Ishii et al., 2000) conducted by voice scientists and physicians, have shown conclusively that the vocal ligament begins to develop in early childhood but does not appear fully intact nor able to function like an adult one until around the age of ten years. This means that registration events specific to singing can't occur until near or after the age of ten years. The precise moment at which the vocal ligament can withstand the antagonism between the muscle pairs involved is not known, and we need to wait until computer simulation studies are undertaken to conclusively pinpoint this moment (Titze, personal correspondence, July 31, 2003). It is very likely that for each child, the precise moment may be different, but based on the voice science studies cited throughout this chapter is likely not to happen before the age of eight years.

Needless to say, this leaves us with a muddled picture of research findings concerned with registration events for singing in very young children (birth to age seven years). Researchers who have suggested that these younger children are using singing registers may have instead documented instances of vocal misuse, such as pressed phonation (Fundamentals of Vocal Health in this chapter), which from a vocal health point makes these studies even more valuable to the research field. Only a healthy voice will be able to develop into one that can efficiently use the vocal singing registers. It is therefore prudent for teachers of young children to encourage healthy vocal behaviors in singing, but not to encourage them to find singing registers they do not yet possess. However, helping older children find these registers when they begin to appear is integral for the development of a healthy singing voice. For more information on encouraging healthy registration events in children's singing voice, the reader is encouraged to review the following excellent materials: Phillips, 1992; Rutkowski, 1986, 1990, 1996; Wassum, 1979; Wurgler, 1990; and Young, 1971.

Learning to Sing Songs

Several stages of singing acquisition seem to occur in American children (Dowling, 1984; Saperston, 1986). In general, the following sequence has been observed: (1) babbling, (2) imitating others and using glissandos, (3) singing discrete pitches then small groups of notes, (4) making up songs and vocalizations, (5) singing parts of songs, but not necessarily with a tonal center, which could be interspersed with made-up songs, (6) singing whole phrases of songs, and (7) singing entire songs with tonal centers maintained.

Young children seem to have an easier time vocalizing descending intervals (Fox, 1990; Michel, 1973; Ramsey, 1983; Ries, 1987; Simons, 1964). Davidson (1985), in observations of children over a six-year period beginning at one year of age, found that children exhibit some consistent behaviors in their acquisition of both standard (learned) and invented songs. In general, they begin with descending intervals of a third, then fourth, then fifth, and then sixth. The patterns begin with leaps and then children fill in the steps between those leaps. While evidence seems to suggest that children sing leaps before steps and that descending motion precedes ascending motion, Sinor (1984) found descending intervals were not always easiest and therefore not the most accurate in pitch. For further and more specific information, see Saperston (1986).

While the described progression suggests a logical sequence of events that happens naturally, it does not take into consideration cultural differences, such as vocal models, value of singing in the culture or family, and encouragement of the vocal behaviors needed for singing to develop. For example, a child who is not encouraged to sing may stagnate in skill development at some point and stop singing. Since the muscle memory required for singing would not be reinforced, the ability to sing songs may be severely compromised. In addition, some differences among cultures regarding song acquisition seem to exist (Chen-Hafteck, 2002). Consequently, while the sequence of song acquisition may be valid, the ages at which children experience these stages may not be universal.

Another difficulty with interpreting these research results is that when investigating song acquisition many researchers look at pitch-matching accuracy or accuracy of intonation. If a child (or any untrained singer) is using a limited singing range and/or an adjustment then the child will not be able to sing in tune when trying to reproduce a song that requires a wider range or use of another adjustment. In fact, children often modulate between keys when singing. While some have interpreted this as a child's inability to maintain a tonal center (Hargreaves, 1996) others acknowledge that children may modulate to accommodate their comfortable singing range (Flowers and Dunne-Sousa, 1990). Therefore, while some trends in learning to sing songs appear to exist, interpretation of these results as conclusive is cautioned.

Table 9.3 Observed Song Acquisition Development

AGES	BEHAVIOR	RESEARCH SOURCES
Birth to 6 months	Babbling with intonation	Fox (1990), Dowling (1984), Michel (1973)
6–12 months	Imitate others	Davidson, McKernon & Gardner (1981), Greenberg (1979), McKernon (1979)
	Mostly descending intervals	Fox (1990), Jersild & Bienstock (1931), Michel (1973), Ries (1987)
12–18 months	Glissandos	Davidson, McKernon & Gardner (1981), Valerio, et al (1988)
18–20 months	Discrete pitches	Davidson, McKernon & Gardner (1981)
18–24 months	Small groups of notes	Davidson, McKernon & Gardner (1981), Gesell & Ilg (1943)
24 months	Sings phrases	Davidson, McKernon & Gardner (1981), Gesell & Ilg (1943)
2–3 years	Sings parts of songs	Dowling (1984), Gesell & Ilg (1943)
3 years +	Sings whole songs	Dowling (1984), Gesell & Ilg (1943), Shuter (1968)

Note: While this behavioral sequence seems consistent among children, the ages at which each child exhibits these behaviors is inconsistent.

Common Myths

Several myths exist about children and singing, including:

1. Girls perform more accurately than boys in a variety of singing tasks. **Not necessarily true**! While some researchers have found that girls sing better than boys (DeCarbo, 1982; Goetze, 1985; Stauffer, 1985; Trollinger, 2001, 2003), the majority of studies that investigated singing differences between boys and girls have found no difference (Cooper, 1992; Kim, 1998; Kirkpatrick, 1962; Runfola, 1981; Rupp, 1992; Rutkowski, 1986; Smale, 1987). It is inappropriate to assume that girls sing better than boys.
2. Good singers have higher music aptitude or ability. **Not true**! Researchers have found little relationship between children's singing ability and music aptitude (Apfelstadt, 1984; Feierabend, 1984; Geringer, 1983; Jarjisian, 1981; Kimble, 1983; Paladino, 1991; Phillips and Aitchison, 1997; Rutkowski, 1986, 1987, 1996; Wang, 1987). The ability to sing is a kinesthetic skill that can be learned (Phillips, 1992), associating singing ability with musicianship, particularly in young children, is erroneous.

3. Only some children can sing. **Not True!** Most children with healthy voices and normal cognitive ability can learn to sing, given the right learning situation.

Issues

Two issues regarding research practice and methodologies when investigating children's singing voices should be raised, specifically concerning physiology and function related to speech and singing development.

1. Many environmental factors (e.g., familial vocal use, native language) influence children's singing development including typical vocal/age ranges of children at or how they learn to sing songs. The research reported is what has been observed of some children. While this information is helpful to teachers of young children, it is not intended to reflect what is normal or natural for all children or what vocal behaviors can be expected in appropriately nurturing environments.

2. Much research with preschool and elementary aged children seems to focus on their ability to sing in tune. While singing in tune is certainly important it should not be an issue of concern until the child has healthy use of the voice. Often children do not sing in tune because they have not developed enough vocal strength to do so or they use the voice inappropriately. *The Singing Voice Development Measure* (SVDM) has been validated as a tool to assess children's use of the voice for singing (author's Web site).

Key Points

The first section of the chapter contains information concerning the nature of the young child's voice, leading to the following.

1. Although infants and preverbal children seem to display a great amount of vocal flexibility that may aid development of singing skills, not all vocal sounds they make will contribute to singing development.

2. The physical mechanisms of young children are anatomically different and less controllable than that of the adult singer.

3. Young children expend more physical energy to speak and sing, since their respiratory systems are underdeveloped.

4. The average singing range of children entering kindergarten seems to be around B3 to A4 (Welch, 1979).

5. Research has not supported a difference between boys and girls' singing ability or that singing is related to musical aptitude or pitch discrimination. In addition, boys' and girls' vocal structures are not different until puberty.

6. Research on how singing generally develops remains inconclusive and difficult to generalize, indicating individual variability in young children's voices.

Application

This section presents the applications of the research and the theories to experiences that will assist adults guiding the vocal development of young children. Also included is guidance to aid assessment of marketed materials and to develop appropriate materials for nurturing children's vocal development and singing. Areas to be addressed include vocal health, vocal models, song materials and selection, instructional settings and activities, teaching songs, and using accompaniments. While some activities are generally appropriate for certain ages, it is most important to base instruction on the child's individual musical and vocal development. The following discussion refers to children's vocal behaviors, not to chronological age.

Fundamentals of Vocal Health

Singing is a strenuous muscular activity and, like other muscles in the body, these muscles and their connective ligaments can be damaged. As the child matures, the problems occurring when young compound. Sataloff (1997) suggests that many bad vocal habits have their roots in infancy. Teachers and parents of young children should be especially aware of the kinds of vocalization habits that may lead to problems, and what to watch and listen for. Although many may think that an unhealthy voice is of no consequence, untreated vocal damage, such as vocal nodules and cysts, negatively affect all vocal behaviors including speech. The voice is not replaceable so it must be treated with the utmost care. There are many skills to aid teachers in instructing voice students. There are two basic skills that anyone working with young voices needs to develop: listening and watching.

How does a teacher or parent know, by listening, that a voice may be damaged? Indicators that something may be wrong commonly include the following sounds:

- A hoarse or rough quality to the voice during speech.
- Two pitches generated simultaneously.
- The vocal sound suddenly stops and returns during speech or singing.
- Abrupt change in normal speech pitch (e.g., suddenly low, not due to illness).

Presence of any of these symptoms requires that a laryngologist or other knowledgeable physician be consulted. None of these vocal behaviors are normal even if a child has exhibited them for a long period of time.

The specific causes of vocal damage are numerous but the ones relevant to this chapter include: (1) singing incorrectly; (2) yelling and screaming; (3) yelling while singing, either because of exuberance or because the song has too wide a range (some children use an inappropriate adjustment to sing the higher pitches); (4) using harsh glottal attacks when singing or speaking (for example, saying "AH" loudly is a glottal attack, and saying "HAH" in a normal voice is not a glottal attack); (5) singing too often and too long without vibrato (for adults); and (6) forcing the voice to speak or sing at a lower level than is natural (more problematic for women than for men). Of special concern is that **a teacher may unknowingly model poor vocal habits and then inadvertently teach them to his or her students**.

Eyes are just as important as ears when working with young voices. Since the voice is located inside the body, it is only normal for the body to react overtly when singing. For example, a child who is singing with a great amount of tension may be (1) standing very stiffly, (2) jutting out the jaw when singing high, (3) pulling the chin in to the chest when singing low, (4) moving the shoulders up and down when taking in a breath for singing (improper clavicular breathing is indicated), (5) not opening the mouth when singing (looks like mumbling), and (6) having the tongue block the entrance to the mouth or throat (one should be able to see clearly into the back of the mouth on vowels "Ah, oh" as the tip of the tongue should stay down on the bottom of the mouth cavity unless making consonants). Teachers of young children need to make sure they are not modeling these behaviors to students when singing.

Good vocal habits for all (teachers and students of both genders) include singing appropriately, not yelling or screaming excessively, and speaking at a comfortable pitch and loudness level. For women, this means that one should not force the voice lower (in the heavy adjustment) in an attempt to sound sexy or authoritative. The larynx continues to drop during life, and a lower voice and greater resonance will naturally develop over time. Forcing it to go there sooner is not advisable. In addition, teachers should not try to sing too high and too loud with a heavy adjustment; a shift to the lighter adjustment should be used. Singing too high and loudly with a heavy adjustment is also known as belting and is not healthy for the voice. Children may be inclined to belt, especially if teachers tell them to "belt it out." A healthy mix of vocal adjustments in the speech voice is desired and physically healthy, and professionally trained voice users in the media do this. Speaking or singing with a sore throat is not recommended. The most important thing anyone can do for the voice is to drink water (not tea, coffee, or soda). Like a car engine needs oil for lubrication, the voice needs lubrication for healthy speaking and singing. The eminent voice scientist, pedagogue and bass, D. Ralph Appelman, sang his final concert in his early seventies and continued to exercise his voice regularly until his death at eighty-six years (R. Appelman, personal correspondence, April 27, 2002).

If a teacher suspects that his/her voice or that of any child shows signs of developing damage, it is imperative to immediately see a voice specialist (speech therapist, laryngologist, or ENT physician), or make this recommendation to the parent of the child. Fortunately, there are many voice clinics, some of them affiliated with universities. Many voice clinics have WebPages offering helpful information. For example, see the National Center for Voice and Speech: <http://www.ncvs.org>; the Voice Foundation: <http://www.voicefoundation.org>; and the National Institute on Deafness and Other Communicative Disorders: <http://www.nidcd.nih.gov>. Finally, professional voice users, such as teachers, will want to monitor their own vocal health carefully.

Steps to Successful Singing Experiences
Pitfalls to Avoid

Do not engage children in vocal activities that will damage the vocal apparatus (physically), possibly permanently. Vocal health needs to be considered before designing any instruction. Songs can inhibit vocal development if not chosen, in range, register, and pitch movement, to reinforce the principles of good singing (Miller, 2000; Titze, 1992; Wurgler, 1990).

Infancy to Four-year-old Children

Very young children's vocal structures are not developed enough to sing complete traditional songs such as the multiple versed *This Old Man*. Children this age should be encouraged to experience flexibility and tonal parameters of the voice, which may prepare them to develop their singing ability as their vocal structures grow and strengthen. Activities include engaging the child in imitative vocal activities (the parent or teacher imitates the child to encourage the desired behavior), spontaneous vocalizing (both parents and child), and babble conversations. Singing to and around children is also important, and it is especially imperative to model healthy vocal habits to the children. When trying to elicit a response from the baby use a lighter adjustment than normal, which more closely matches the baby's vocal timbre. It is by attending to and imitating parents' and caregiver's vocalizations that infants learn to vocalize, speak, and sing.

Verbal Children/Older Preschool (Four Years and Above)

Appropriate Vocal Models

Research indicates that a light adjustment model elicits more light adjustment responses among children (Rupp, 1992), a female model elicits more accurate responses than a male model (Sims, Moore, and Kuhn, 1982), and a child model seems to be the best (Green, 1987). There appears to be no difference between boys and girls in their responses to these models (Kim, 1998). Singing with a focused pitch is also important, and research suggests that singing without vibrato to the children will provide that focus (Yarbrough et al., 1992). However, encouraging adult teachers to sing using this straight-tone is vocally unhealthy, as it creates a great amount of vocal tension (essentially, the vocal bands become more like Popsicle sticks than rubber bands) and sets the stage for vocal damage. Teachers who model without vibrato should do so carefully and only as needed, and never on a regular basis.

Selecting Songs for Singing

Research has provided some guidance in the musical characteristics that make a song easier for some children to sing. Whereas one should take these characteristics into consideration when selecting songs for children, one should ultimately base song selection on the singing abilities of the children. Some three-year-olds with more developed singing ability may be able to sing more musically complex songs than older children. However, the following basic criteria should be considered when selecting songs for young children to sing: (1) sing songs with words; (2) sing songs without words (use a syllable such as boo, bah, boh, and bow with very young singers to encourage clear and stress-free onsets. Using syllables such as those starting with "z" or "m" are also excellent but will be best used with older children who are able to do so without clenching their jaws); (3) use songs with short repetitive phrases; (4) use songs in an appropriate range: within D4 to A4 is generally considered the optimal range, at least to start; (5) use descending intervals, for example in the song, *Nanny Goat* (author's Web site); and (6) use descending skipping patterns such as "just choose me" in *Bickle Bockle* (authors Web site). Songs should not be selected using adult tastes and criteria (e.g., country-western, opera, pop, musical theater), since those songs are meant for adult voices to sing. If songs require a leap upwards into the upper register, usually above A4, it is recommended that the melody leap above that pitch and descend to it rather than climbing up step-wise to reach it (Wurgler, 1990). Finally, even with the criteria in mind, the teacher should try to provide as much variety as possible in song styles, with the realization that as children's voices grow, their ability to sing more complex and diverse songs will also improve.

Selecting Songs for Listening

Children learn to sing and be musical much like they learn a language. It would be ludicrous to suggest that children could learn a language if they never heard it! This is one reason why providing a good vocal model beginning in infancy is important. The following criteria are suggested: (1) live singing is better than recorded singing (important in providing a visual model as well as an aural one), (2) use a variety of songs and song styles, and (3) use recordings of men judiciously (some children will try to sing along in the same range as the male singer, which may cause them to use their voices in an unhealthy manner).

Instructional Settings and Experiences

It is becoming increasingly clear that the instructional setting for young children should be unstructured. Young children learn by playing and being immersed in rich and varied environments (Gordon, 1997; Tarnowski, 1994, 1999; Valerio et al., 1988). Older children (typically four or five years old) may be ready for more structured experiences that are usually associated with school. The type of instructional setting provided for children should be based on children's singing and musical development, not chronological age. When children are singing complete songs on their own they are usually ready for more structured settings. However, use caution when designing structured instructional strategies much before the age of four.

Providing Appropriate Unstructured Musical/Singing Environments

Research has provided evidence that rich musical environments contribute to children's ability to sing (Kirkpatrick, 1962; Apfelstadt, 1984; Wendrich, 1981). Rich musical environments are those that include adults singing to children, encouraging children to learn songs correctly (when age appropriate), playing singing games with children, teaching nursery rhymes, having conversations with children in song or making up songs, purchasing recordings of children's songs and stories, and family participation in musical activities (Kirkpatrick, 1962). The emphasis for infants and toddlers should be to help them develop good vocal habits that they can build upon to develop singing skills, which are more strenuous. Good habits should be reinforced as children learn to sing.

Providing Appropriate Structured Musical/Singing Environments

When children are at least four years old and can comfortably sing complete songs, they may be ready for more structured singing activities. These types of activities are numerous and are included in various sources on the author's Web site. Some general strategies and a few structured activities include (1) teach a song by rote, (2) provide immediate feedback to the children, in a nurturing manner, (3) play musical games that encourage children to sing alone and in small groups, and (4) encourage them to sing as a group and listen to each other. Some who work with children's voices adamantly believe that teachers should not sing with their students. There are times however, when singing with the students is important (e.g., when helping them get over a difficult passage, or to model an appropriate vocal behavior precisely at the moment it is required and needs to be reinforced). If the teacher sings with the children, use a gradual fading out (and not singing loudly) until the children can sing by themselves.

Teaching Songs

There are generally two approaches to teaching songs, via immersion or via rote. **Immersion** learning will generally happen in an unstructured environment, and the children will learn the song by hearing it over and over. This method of teaching a song is best for the very youngest children. When children are a bit older, they can learn short songs by **rote,** which is an "I sing a phrase/you sing it back" approach. Information on teaching a song by rote is available in most elementary music methods books, and is also a cornerstone of Kodály methodology (Chapter 6).

Using Accompaniment

It is likely that children learn a song best without accompaniment but with the teacher or other live music as a vocal model. The children should not depend on an accompaniment to teach them a song. However, after the song is learned, it is appropriate to use piano accompaniment or a recorded accompaniment as long as the children are not placed in a situation where they must force their voices to be heard over the accompaniment.

Examples of Singing Experiences

The following are suggestions for unstructured activities that develop good vocal and singing habits. These include but are not limited to: (1) engage in musical dialogues with all children, (2) chant and sing short patterns to and with the children, (3) improvise tunes (child vocalizes, parent responds: parent vocalizes, child responds), (4) animate stories using character voices (but be careful to not go too low), and (5) let a child create a song and teach it to parent, teacher, or classmates. For more information, readers are encouraged to review methods in Chapter 6. The following two experiences build vocal flexibility and range through improvisation and imitation.

1. *Musical dialogues (use the voice to chant and sing: infant and older).* Listen when the child vocalizes and imitate the sounds the child makes. Match their pitches to encourage them to repeat the vocalization. This can be a game, and very young infants can even learn to match a pitch the parent sings (Wendrich, 1981), as long as it is in the comfortable vocalization range of the child's voice. Think of this as having a musical dialogue with the child.

2. *Create tunes (Improvise tunes to accompany play: after first year and above).* Encourage children to make up tunes of their own, then sing them back to them. Again, turn this into a game. The tunes may be very short, perhaps only two notes, but it's a start.

Summary and Key Points

The best way to help children develop healthy voices is to provide **appropriate models** for them. Just as children learn language through spoken models, then, they learn music and how to sing through the musical models provided.

1. Adults should sing in a light voice, with females always above middle C (C4), when modeling for children. Males should sing above C3, paralleling the female voice at an octave lower. A light falsetto, which would place the male voice at the same pitch level as an adult female or child, may be helpful for the very young, especially for those children having trouble using their singing voices.

2. Children need to be sung to just as they are spoken to, so use musical dialogues with children that include patterns and songs with and without words.
3. Children need to experience a variety of vocal music, not just commercially available music for children.
4. Songs to be sung by children should be short, of limited range, not go lower than D4, not have too many phrases that move up by step, and not leap up to notes higher than A4.
5. Children should be encouraged to explore their voices through sound animations and with songs that are higher and have wider ranges.
6. Children should be given opportunities to sing individually as well as in groups.

10

Experiences: Moving and Creating

Children are predisposed to move to the sound of music. They spontaneously move to recorded and live music. Emile Jaques-Dalcroze believed that rhythm is the primary element in music and the source for all musical rhythm may be found in the natural rhythms of the human body (e.g., heartbeat, a newborn's sucking rate, and rhythm of breathing) (Fraisse, 1982). Dalcroze identified the body as the first instrument to be trained in music.

Children usually experience some form of musical movement in the schools. They move to recordings, their own music making, the teacher's performances, physical education movement, and dance movement. Movement is a concrete way to learn about music. Bruner has suggested three possible ways (enactive, iconic, and symbolic) in which experiences are translated into a personal model of the world. Children respond better to doing than to abstract language or pictorial representation. Movement to music is an enactive or concrete mode of learning and helps the child internalize music concepts outlined in Chapter 7 such as fast/slow, high/low, even/uneven, longer/shorter, and moving up/moving down.

Movement Research

Issues

The Early Childhood Music and Movement Association (ECMMA), is devoted to the ideal that all children should be given the advantage of music and movement instruction from birth to age seven (ECMMA, 2002). Although movement and music experiences work well with young children, there are still many classrooms that have inadequate space for movement or teachers who do not choose to use movement. The seventeenth-century philosopher René Descartes, famous for the idea, "I think; therefore I am," promoted the concept of mind and body being separate. The mind versus body dualism promulgated by Descartes has gradually given way to holistic ideas about how humans learn and how the brain works. Current neuroscience research underlines how every part of the body is connected to the brain (Flohr and Hodges, 2002). In a sense, the brain is a network of neural pathways throughout the body with a central control residing in the head. For example, movement with the feet is connected to a central controller, the brain, and promotes learning. The child will get it or makes the connection between action (e.g., movement) and music. In movement, as with all experiences with young children, it is important to remember individual differences. For some children a rhythm experience may be too demanding or not challenging enough. For example, most three- and four-year-olds find skipping demanding. Child-centered education practices and developmentally appropriate experiences accommodate these individual differences.

Theories

This section briefly describes the ideas of Dalcroze, Weikart, and Metz. Dalcroze believed that humans feel emotion by various sensations produced at different levels of muscular contraction and relaxation. The muscular contraction-relaxations of emotion are analogous to the the tension and release of music. In answer to the question of what gives music life and expression, he wrote, "Movement, rhythm" (Jaques-Dalcroze, 1921, p. 101). He summarizes an essay on the initiation into rhythm with a list of eight conclusions. Notice that Dalcroze believed that rhythm includes much more than steady beat, eighth notes, quarter notes, and short rhythm patterns. He underlines the flowing quality of rhythm and movement: (1) Rhythm is movement; (2) Rhythm is essentially physical; (3) Every movement involves time and space; (4) Musical consciousness is the result of physical experience; (5) The perfecting of physical resources results in clarity of perception; (6) The perfecting of movements in time assures consciousness of musical rhythm; (7) The perfecting of movements in space assures consciousness of plastic rhythm; (8) The perfecting of movements in time and space can only be accomplished by exercises in rhythmic movement (Jaques-Dalcroze, 1921, p. 83). His ideas and method also were discussed in Chapter 6.

Phyllis Weikart (1998) brings ideas from of kinesiology to musical movement (Chapter 6). Key movement experiences for the preschooler are (1) acting on movement directions, (2) describing movement, (3) moving in nonlocomotor and (4) locomotor ways (including moving to music), (5) moving with objects, (6) expressing creativity, (7) feeling and expressing steady beat, and (8) moving in sequences to a common beat (Weikart and Carlton, 1995).

She has developed a sequence for identifying and demonstrating the steady beat or pulse of the music (Weikart, 1998, pp. 30–31, 68). The steps in her Four-Step Language Process lead to the ability to feel and maintain the steady beat or pulse of the music and are useable with children above preschool age. Weikart recommends only the second step for preschoolers (P. Weikart, personal correspondence, June 6, 2002).

1. SAY—Speak slowly the word that best describes the action, or chant, "BEAT, BEAT, BEAT, BEAT" without movement or music.
2. SAY and DO—Slowly speak the word BEAT four times, and then accompany the word with the movement (all without music). Note: preschoolers should begin the movement four times in a slow tempo, and then attach the word that best describes the action or body part. This step creates the cognitive-motor link.

3. WHISPER and DO—the word is whispered so thought is retained. When music is added, thinking aids attention which is a necessary component for maintaining a steady beat to the music.
4. THINK and DO—Thought is retained while attending to the feel of the underlying steady beat of music.

Weikart explains that children three to five years of age should not be asked to count repetitions of movement while moving (counting repetitions alone is appropriate). Doing two things at once is not within the abilities of most children at this age. Weikart (1990) believes children younger than seven should not be asked to move to an alternating sequence (two movements on one side of the body before the same two movements on the other side) because those movements are not developmentally appropriate.

Metz (1989) developed a theory of movement responses to music using three core categories. The first, conditions, involves three preexisting individual qualities of behavioral disposition, developmental stage, and mode of representation. The second, interactions, contains overt behaviors of the children and teacher that influence movement to music. These behaviors include child or teacher modeling, describing, and suggesting. The third, outcomes, involves the contextual environmental properties of music responses and nonmusic-related responses.

Developmental Milestones for Moving

Milestones in Table 10.2 are set to approximate ages. Individual children differ widely; their skills generally improve with age, experience, and instruction.

The work of Moog (1976a, 1976b) has implications for movement development including: an increase in the number of coordinated movements by age three, more complexity at age four, and a decrease in spontaneous movements between four and six years as children clap more to the music (see Table 10.1). There are milestones in development for motor skills (Table 10.2). For example, there are at least thirteen milestones in the development of general locomotion skills: rolling, crawling, creeping, cruising (one hand on object), walking, jumping, running, hopping, climbing, sliding, galloping, dodging, and skipping (Jansma and French, 1994). Each of the locomotive milestones has subskills.

Keeping the steady beat is also referred to as synchronization to the beat of music or matching the heartbeat of music. The abbreviation **bpm** (beats per minute) or **m.m.** (metronome marking) is used to describe the speed of the beat. Both bpm and m.m. refer to the number of steady beats during a minute.

The ability to keep a steady beat is basic to musical performance. This ability is affected by the interaction of age, type of instrument or movement used, individual differences, whether with music or without music, tempo of the music, and culture. It is too simplistic to say all four-year-olds prefer a tempo of 130 bpm.

Table 10.1 Selected Movement Research and Reviews

AUTHOR	AGE	N	SUMMARY OF SELECTED FINDINGS
Moog (1976ab)	.5–5.5	500	From birth to 1.6 years the child develops from showing pleasure and slight movement to bouncing, swaying, and conducting. After 1.6 years Moog noticed a decrease in movement and an increase in the variety of movements. The number of coordinated movements increases by age 3. Around age 4 the movements become more complex. During the ages 4–6 the spontaneous movements decrease and the children more often clap to the music.
Loong (2002)	1.1–5	60	Response depends on instrument played. Tempi ranged from 111–168 bpm.
Metz (1989)	2–4	60	Free-choice participation setting. Three theoretical core categories emerged from data analysis: conditions, interactions, and outcomes. Generated a theory of children's movement responses to music. Describes seven propositions for application to movement in early childhood. Younger children imitated their peers more than older children. Teacher modeling may be more effective than peer modeling. Modeling with describing and suggesting increased music-related responses.
Flohr & Brown (1979)	3–5	79	In two studies peer imitation significantly influenced expressive movement. More imitation occurred for 5-year-olds during listening to unfamiliar music.
Rainbow (1981)	3–5	154	Children found marching and marching while clapping very difficult. Only four children were 5 year olds.
Flohr, Suthers, & Woodward (1998)	3–8	245	Children from Australia, South, Africa, and the U.S. Differences were found for gender, age, and success in the way in which the steady beat was performed. Older children performed better. Girls outperformed the boys. All were better at steady beat for tempi 110–130 bpm. The most difficult was 150 bpm. Most successful at patschen and least successful at marching.
Frego (1996)	4–12	158	Large motor locomotion. Faster walking and marching tempi from 4–6 years. Then a gradual decline in speed through age 12.
Patrick (1998)	4–6	72	Movement participation increased when children utilized a prop. Evidence of peer imitation was noted during the no prop sessions.
Tsapakidou, Zachopoulou & Zographou (2001)	4–6	60	After a three-month movement program, children improved their space awareness and their readiness through motor responses to auditory stimuli. Their rhythmic coordination and rhythmic synchronization were better after the experimental procedure. Also, children gave more movement solutions to motor problems presented by the teacher.
Walters (1983)	5–8	96	Small motor tapping. The mean personal tempo for all subjects was 106.8 bps, but the range was from 114.6 for K's to 99.5 in third grade. Children found it more difficult to synchronize movement with music that is different from their personal tempo.
Jordan-DeCarbo & Nelson (2002)	Review	Review	Review of research in early childhood, pp. 210–242. Movement, p. 222.

Table 10.2   Milestones in Motor Skill Development

MONTHS	MILESTONE
2–3	Unsteady and generalized movement to music. Engages in bouncing, tapping, and tickling music experiences. Able to shake small maracas and rattles. Puts small instruments in mouth.
5	When lying prone, rests weight on hands with chest off ground.
6	Rolls from back to stomach. Uses pincer grasp with small rhythm instruments.
7	Maintains erect sitting position.
8	Stands and briefly maintains balance. May use three different hand movements to respond to music. Bounces up and down while standing (supported).
10	Creeps on hands and knees; uses rail of crib to pull self up. Imitates facial movements of person in close proximity who is singing.
12	Walks forward and backward. Bounces and rocks to music while standing. Imitates movements never before performed in music activities.
15	Creeps up two steps. Imitates movements of another child.
18	Throws a ball. Walks and seldom falls. Increase in variety of movements to music. Enjoys shaking maracas to fast tempi (160+ bpm). The child is able to start and stop movement with music. Able to bounce (bend at knees) and rock from one foot to the other. Not many children put instruments in their mouths at 18 months.
21	Kicks a ball after demonstration.
24	Runs well, but not fast, without falling. Teacher or parent should try to match the child's movement with a drum or other instrument to find child's preferred tempo. Will move almost immediately to music with a steady beat.
30	Walks on tiptoes after demonstration. Jumps up with both feet off floor after demonstration. May also tiptoe and jump to music.
33	Jumps off low platform.
36	Will respond to call and response task with movements. Imitates arm swinging across midline (e.g., swings left arm across middle to the right side of body). Chanting may be easiest way to show steady beat. May be able to clap or play sticks to the beat. Will participate in simple circle games with movement. Begin giving children a repertoire of movements to music.
42	Walks on a walking board. Imitates movements of peers and adults. May invent movements.
48	Jumps while running. Skips with one foot forward. One-third of the children may be able to skip (Frego, 1998). One-foot balance. Movement to music more complex. Spontaneous movements decrease and children often clap to the music. Able to perform simple movement experiences using arm swings, twisting, hammering fists, and shaking hands in front (see experiences 3–6 below). Children's walking or stepping tempo usually 130–140 bpm.
54	Hops on one foot.
60	Skips alternating lead foot. Two-thirds of the children may be able to skip (Frego, 1998). Catches balls and other objects. May engage in simple folk dances.
72	Children's walking or stepping tempo increased to peak of 149 bpm and then gradually slows to 134 bpm at 11–12 years (Frego).

Adapted with musical examples from (Jansma & French, 1994). © Prentice Hall. Used by Permission.

Steady beat

1. *Age*—As children grow older, they are on average, better able to keep the steady beat to music (Flohr, 2000; Frego, 1996; Malbrán, 2002).

2. *Type of instrument or movement task*—Loong (2002) found the average tempo performed by sixty young children aged five years and below was 112 bpm for scraping/rubbing, 132 bpm for walking/stepping, 141 bpm for striking, and 164 bpm for shaking a maraca. It is easier for young children to keep the steady beat using certain movements (e.g., chanting or tapping) than other movements (e.g., marching) (Flohr, Suthers, and Woodward, 1998; Frega, 1979; Rainbow, 1981; Schleuter and Schleuter, 1985). Rainbow and Frega reported that matching the steady beat while marching and marching while clapping to music was extremely difficult for three- and four-year-olds. Rainbow found only 10 to 14 percent of three-year-olds were successful at clapping a pattern or a steady beat to recorded music. The easiest steady beat task for three- and four-year-olds was chanting rhythm syllables (e.g., rat–a–tat–tat or ta–ta–titi–ta) without use of movement. In light of the research, a developmentally **in**appropriate practice would be to expect three- and four-year-olds to march or march while clapping because most of them will not be able to do so. However, young children enjoy moving to music (including marching to music) and the experiences are viable as long as teachers and parents do not expect them to match the steady beat until six or seven years of age. Experience of teachers indicates that if you instruct the children to stay with the beat and model the behavior, they do better than if you just tell them to move.

3. *Individual differences*—Tempo preference is often identified as personal tempo and refers to the natural tempo that exists within an individual. Personal tempo can often be determined by asking the child to move without listening to music. The preferred tempo or personal tempo generally decreases as the child ages (Frego, 1996; Walters, 1983). Frego found that there was an increase in the personal tempo of walking speed between five and six years of age but that the peak tempo of 149 bpm at first grade gradually decreased to 134 bpm in sixth grade.

4. *Tempo*—Young children keep the steady beat more easily if the beat is close to their preferred or personal tempo (Smoll and Schutz, 1978; Walters, 1983). Vaughn observed "[S]tart with a tempo dictated by the children's own behavior and their ability to respond will increase dramatically" (Vaughan, 1981). Rainbow (1981) found many activities were difficult for three- and four-year-olds. However, Rainbow used a tempo of 104 bpm for marching whereas the average preferred marching tempo of three- and four-year-old children is close to 139 bpm (Frego, 1996). Rainbow might have elicited a different response had he used a faster tempo.

5. *Culture*—There is evidence that a child's cultural surroundings influence the ability to keep the steady beat to music (Flohr et al., 1998; Rose, 1995; Vaughan, 1981). For example, Rose (1995) found that children raised in a mountain culture where a dance called clogging was common were better at keeping the beat than children from a city environment

Steps to Successful Moving Experiences

Pitfalls to Avoid

The major pitfall to avoid is possible injury to a child. As children move to music they can become very excited. Set up the room for movement. Remove or place padding on all furniture and other objects that may injure a child (e.g., sharp corner of a piano). Make sure there is enough space for the type of movement being used. Each child should have personal space in which to move.

Steps

- *Set the environment and boundaries for movement.* Whether the children move to the music while still in their chairs or move through a room, it is advisable to set the environment to reflect boundaries for movement. Many movements to music may be done with limited space using only arms, hands, and head. Encourage positive experiences by setting rules for moving (stop/start with the music, respect each other's space).
- *Stop and Start.* Do **not** start children moving around the room before you are able to control them. First work with the children until they are used to stopping and starting with the music.
- *Use the many available ways to incorporate movement.* Basic elements of the music movement program for young children are feeling the beat, expressing the beat, synchronizing the beat, time/space awareness, expressive movement to music, and creative movement. Below is a listing of general movement experiences.

Action songs.   Movements (embedded in the text) accompany a song such as *Wheels on the Bus Go Round and Round* or *If You're Happy and You Know It, Clap Your Hands.*

Dance.   Movement formalized into dances with simple patterns. For example, formalized movements to *Hop Old Squirrel* are appropriate for four- to six-year-olds (author's Web site).

Describe a Movement.   Talk about movements the children make. Also describe animal movements.

Move to the beat and Expressive Movement.   Expressing music through move-ment. For example, *Show me the way music moves.*

Movement with props.   Many objects may be used as a movement prop, for example stick horses, scarves, puppets, or plastic aquarium figures (Patrick, 1998).

Movement with single sounds.   Move to isolated sound sources. For example, play a drum and ask the children to move their arms until they do not hear the drum any longer. Then play a triangle and move for the duration of the sound. Notice how much longer the triangle sound lasts. Use other instruments and found sound sources.

Sequences.   Several movement songs have number or word sequences. For example, *Owls in a Tree* (author's Web site) sequences numbers, and *Bought Me a Cat* sequences animals and their sounds (Smith and Leonhard, 1968). Other music describes events. For example, in Grieg's *Morning from Peer Gynt* (NARAS, 1999) the music describes a sunrise. Children could be asked to represent through their movements the sequence of events during the morning sunrise. There are also musical sequences where a pattern is repeated higher or lower. For example, in *Shoo Fly* (Smith and Leonhard, 1968), the phrase "Flies in the buttermilk, shoo fly, shoo" is sung three times (the second time is sung lower than the first and the last time is sung like the first phrase).

Singing game movement.   Many singing games incorporate movements such as passing (*Tisket Tasket*), creating movements (*Hey, Hey, Look at Me*), and moving around the group (*Nanny Goat*) (author's Web site).

- *Wiggles, tickles, and tapping.*   Feierabend (2000a) has collected and recorded many good experiences for young children (see experiences, below).

- *Word stimulus/interpretative movement.*   Moving to descriptive words or phrases such as "Move as if you are a flower" or "Move like an elephant."

- *Tempo.* Select music of many tempi designed to match the preferences of the children in the classroom. Try grouping children into groups based on their *personal tempo.* Ability to keep the steady beat is affected by the interaction of age, type of instrument or movement used, individual differences, whether with music or without hearing music, tempo of the music, and culture.

Examples of Moving Experiences

Experiences with music and movement should be at the center of young children's music education. Movement experiences are also a very fertile ground for creating. A rich resource of prekindergarten experiences is the Sims publication based on the national music education standards (Sims, 1995, pp. 32–52). Feelings and the expressiveness of music may be united with movement. Use a variety of recorded music, improvised music, and rhythm instruments to supply the music for move-ment. Each experience needs a clear objective).

1. *Tapping the beat (Move to music: infant).*
    Tapping the beat with an infant or toddler is a game shared by adults and babies (Feierabend, 2000b) (see Chapter 6). For example, the steady beat of the music is reinforced as the parent or caregiver moves their fingers up the child's arm.
    Slowly, Slowly
    Slowly, Slowly (chant with a steady beat while moving fingers)
    Slowly, slowly, very slowly
    With one finger, slowly draw a circle in baby's palm
    Creeps the garden snail.
    Slowly, slowly, very slowly
    With one finger, walk up baby's arm
    Up the wooden rail.
    Quickly, quickly, very quickly
    With one finger, quickly draw a circle in baby's palm
    Runs the little mouse.
    Quickly, quickly, very quickly
    With one finger, walk up baby's arm
    In his little house.
    (Feierabend, 2000a, p. 45. Used by permission of G.I.A. publications.)
    Feierabend describes more tapping techniques (he also calls them tickling).
2. *Move to the music for infants (Move to music: birth through two years).*
    Dance with the child: hold him or her close and gently move to the rhythm and tempo of the music. As the baby matures, supply the legs for a non-walker to dance; put his or her feet on your feet and dance or march to the beat.
3. *Accent game (Move to show changes in music: two to six years).*
    Start children walking around room with a soft drum beat or piano music. Play a heavily accented beat (much louder) and the children will usually jump a little. Ask them to think of walking in the rain and when the loud accent occurs, jump over a puddle or curb. Group the accents into even groups of two, four, and eight and then omit the accent. Notice how the children will expect the accent and jump. Change where the accent occurs to develop listening skill.
4. *Show me the way the music moves (Move to show changes in music: three to six years).*
    Start with children seated. Use short excerpts of one or two minutes for the younger children. Ask the children to show the way the music moves with their head, hands, and arms. Demonstrate a few movements to the music. The goal is to encourage moving the body in a way that is analogous to the way the music moves. After the children are familiar with the piece of music, get up and move through space with larger movements that employ the entire body.

5. *Concept machine (Move to show changes in music: three to six years).*
   Use a movable chalkboard or a box as the opposite machine. Students enter one side of the machine showing a musical concept by the way they move, for example, they enter the opposite machine moving fast. Inside the opposite machine they are changed and exit moving to illustrate the opposite of the musical concept—in this example, moving slowly. The use of recorded or improvised music accompaniments for the concepts will provide a creating experience for children improvising. Possible concepts include shorter/longer, even/uneven, faster/slower, higher/lower, and louder/softer. For the older ages and after the children are acclimated to the game, give a child or group of children a slip of paper showing a pair of opposites such as shorter/longer. The child or group moves through the opposite machine and the class decides what concepts are being shown.

6. *Big Foot or Hairy Mammoth Game (Move to music durations: three to six years).*
   Big Foot is a controlled tag game. The teacher controls the rhythm. Use this game only with children who have learned to stop and start with the music so that control is maintained when the music stops in the game. Begin playing a drum beat for the children and ask them to move through space with a steady march tempo, quarter or step = 139 or 140 bpm (the approximate preferred marching tempo for three- and four-year-olds). Decrease the speed by half (half note) and then increase the speed to twice as fast (eighth note). To stimulate the children's interest use a visual picture of animals for each speed. The visual pictures should be images within the child's experience. For example, use little mice feet for 280 bpm (very, very fast!), a marching band for 140 bpm, and big foot or the hairy mammoth from the current animated movie *Ice Age* for 70 bpm. Start the tag game (no tags back). Use a piece of cloth or a hat to identify the person who is **it**. The rule is everyone in the game can only move to the drumbeat. Stop the beat if the children are not moving with the beat. The children will quickly learn how to use time and space to take larger steps in order to catch another child.

7. *Beat motions: Child initiated beat motions (Move to music: four and five years).*
   Children stand in circle. One at a time each child selects some chore and shows a motion to represent that chore. All children imitate that motion and together they sing the song at the appropriate tempo to reflect the motion while keeping the steady beat (Feierabend, 2000c). Used by permission of G.I.A. Publications.

   Include child initiated and teacher initiated activities in every lesson. For example, asking the children to follow your hand-clapping beat is teacher initiated. Allowing a child to initiate the steady beat is a child initiated activity.

Figure 10.1 *Do, do, pity my case*

Teacher initiated beat tempo should stay between 120 and 136 beats per minute.

Introduction to Creating

Of all the music experiences for young children, creative experiences are the least used in classrooms. Unfortunately, creativity is often vaguely viewed as some mysterious talent. Parents and teachers think of singing, movement, listening to recordings, and playing instruments before creative activities. Experiences offered in this chapter can assist encouragement of music creating.

What is creativity? Certainly creating involves the ability to generate new innovative ideas or products that are useful and valued by others. Young children often improvise music in their free play. Improvisation is a spontaneous invention and shaping of music. Folkestad (1998, p. 109) points out that time is a key distinction between improvisation and composition. The spontaneous invention of music exists in real time and may be called an instant composition. In addition, its creator performs the improvisation. A musical composition may be separated from its creator and performed by others. A music composition involves creating music that is finalized in some way, for example, written with a notational system so another person or group can perform it. Improvisation and composition are both creative; this chapter focuses on improvisation.

Two kinds of experiences, free exploration and guided exploration facilitate improvisation. In free exploration the child is left alone to explore instruments, the voice, pots and pans, or any other sound-making object in the environment. In guided exploration, the teacher or parent serves as a guide to the child's exploration by asking questions or engaging in parallel play with the child. Active exploration and interaction is a part of the NAEYC appropriate practice guidelines and the MENC standards (Bredekamp, 1987; MENC, 1994a).

Children enjoy and engage in improvising music with their voices and instruments. Any experienced parent or teacher of young children will agree with Gardner's (1982) portrayal of the preschool years as characterized by creative behavior. "Play provides a safe place to try on the roles of others, to fantasize, and to explore new ideas. Children's play involves imitation and improvisation" (Sims, 1995, p. 91). Young children may learn about music and a host of subjects more effectively through creative play than any other way (Gardner, 1982; Piaget, 1962). Further information about music creativity may be found in several works (Campbell, 1991; Colwell and Richardson, 2002; Kratus, 1991, in press; Sundin, McPherson, and Folkestad, 1998; Stauffer, 1999, 2001; Webster, 1987).

Research

Issues

Young children are clearly creative and musical creativity is an important field for research. Fortunately, several studies of young children's musical creativity have been completed during the past two decades (Sundin et al., 1998). There are four caveats to consider. First, much of the creativity research deals with children older than six years, the research about children above seven years is provided here as a contrast to what the younger children can do. Second, much of the literature is about the importance of music play (free and guided exploration) and the description of children's music play. Literature during the past decade includes a refined measurement of creative thinking (Webster, 1992), one compilation from Sweden (Sundin et al., 1998), and a new mini-series book about composition (Kratus, in press). Third, the research definitions of creative activities are in conflict. For example, improvisation is usually treated as instant music where its creator performs the improvisation. By contrast, Swanwick and Tilman (1986) write about composition to include improvisation. Fourth, some studies report on only vocal creating while others examine only instrumental creating.

Theories

The field of psychology has spawned a number of ideas and theories about creativity. This brief overview examines four theories: Guilford, Sternbery, and Lubart, and Webster.

Guilford's concept of creativity is defined with a model structure of intellect including 120 factors across three dimensions. The three dimensions are operations, what the child does; contents, the vehicle (for example, the musical instruments); and products, the forms in which the information is processed. Guilford's influential work includes the ideas of **divergent** and **convergent** thinking. Divergent thinking results when the teacher or parent asks a child for many possible answers to one question. Divergent thinking concepts include fluency (number of different responses), flexibility (different classes of responses), originality (novelty of responses), and elaboration (extension of responses). Convergent thinking is that which results in a single best or correct answer to one question. In divergent thinking a teacher may ask the children to think of many different ways of moving to a piece of music. In convergent thinking, the teacher may ask the children to find the best single way to move to the piece of music.

Table 10.3 Selected Creativity Research and Reviews

AUTHOR	AGE	N	SUMMARY OF SELECTED FINDINGS
Trollinger (1978)	0–6	74	Fathers of highly creative women (HCW) attended more cultural events such as concerts, lectures, and theaters. Families of HCW attended concerts, other cultural events, and traveled together. HCW began music lessons earlier in life (74% by the age of six as opposed to 40% of the lesser creative).
Pillsbury Foundation Studies (1978)	2–6+	20+	Observation of spontaneous creative behavior. In general, young children not predisposed to make pretty, symmetrical tunes, but rather patterns, shapes, and structures whose elements are rhythmic figures and intervals.
Flohr (1985)	2–5	40	Longitudinal study. Three continuous levels of improvisation were identified. Level 1, motor energy, was characterized by plodding and accented durations (pendulum-like regularity). Similar to scribbling in art. Level 2, experimentation: the child experiments with his or her own capacity for sound production. Level 3, formal properties, is characterized by repetition, large formal structures, and decentered perception.
Tilman & Swanwick (1989)	3–11	40+	Spiral development. By age 9 creating in vernacular mode (cultural influences).
Shelley (1981)	3–5	30	Followed Pillsbury studies observation of free exploration. Several factors seemed to encourage creativity (beautiful sounding instruments, support environment, free exploration within structure, and encouragement of teachers who observed and sometimes participated).
Smithrim (1997)	4	8	Behaviors during free play would not have occurred during teacher-led activities (for example group singing, group moving). Behaviors included spontaneous games, sound exploration, long periods of absorbed activity, unconventional use of instruments, and teaching peers. Children more likely to imitate peers than follow peer instructions.
Flohr (1981)	5	29	Short-term music instruction including improvisation influenced children's developmental music aptitude measured by Gordon's PMMA.
Davies (1992)	5–7	32	Collected songs. The urge to make meaning drives the child's developmental process. Found four bar phrases, used repetition and alternation, borrowed motives from other song material.
Webster (1987)	Review	Review	Creative behavior not necessarily related to music aptitude. Proposed a conceptual model of creative thinking in music (pp. 161–2.) Measure of creative thinking for 7- to 10-year-olds (MTCM).
Webster (1992)	Review	Review	Review of literature on creativity and assessment of creativity.
Sundin, McPherson & Folkestad (1998)	Review	Review	Review of general creativity.
Colwell & Richardson (2002)	Review	Review	See Chapters 11 (Improvisation), 14 (Early childhood), and 23 (Creativity).
Kratus; Stauffer (in press)	Review	Review	Prentice Hall mini-series books on composing and improvising.

Webster (1987; 1990; 1992) provides reviews of musical creativity. He developed a theory of creative thinking in music that works with his assessment instrument, MMCT (see author's Web site). His theory utilizes the idea of divergent thinking as it interacts with convergent thinking. Besides the quantity of ideas a child might create, Webster's theory includes flexibility and originality. For example, when given a xylophone to explore, some children will try to reproduce a song such as *Twinkle, Twinkle, Little Star,* some will improvise on a known song, and others will create original and ever-changing improvisations.

Sternberg and Lubart (1996) have developed components of creativity that are part of an investment theory. A variety of intellectual resources—knowledge, cognitive style, personality, environmental, and motivational—combine to stimulate creativity. For example, a supportive environment serves to stimulate and promote special talents in music (Monsaas and Engelhard, 1990; Trollinger, 1978). The investment theory is promising for its ability to suggest instructional strategies such as good environment and motivation incentives for children.

Developmental Sequences—Improvisation

The work of Pond and others at the Pillsbury Foundation is an early study about musical improvisations of young children (Moorehead and Pond, 1978). Pond found that young children playing instruments and singing were not predisposed to make pretty, symmetrical tunes, but rather patterns, shapes, and structures whose elements are rhythmic figures and intervals. After the pioneering work of Pond other studies examined the nature of improvisation activities. Cohen (1980) and Shelley (1981) followed the naturalistic techniques of the Pillsbury studies and observed three- to five-year-old children's free explorations. The qualitative research of Cohen involved observation of kindergarten children's musical behavior in an unstructured music center. The study concluded that children's free exploration of instruments in an unstructured situation might be categorized under the headings of mastery and the generating of musical gestures. Intensive analysis of the gestures produced indicated that kinesthetic (movement) gestures are the source of musical gestures. Cohen found that children's improvisations including the gestures (or musical phrases and sentences) were dominated by ways the child moved. Until such time as children can produce pure musical gestures, they produce hybrids in which kinesthetic components compensate for aspects for which the child can not yet produce an acoustic analogue. Through observation of free exploration Shelley identified several factors that seemed to encourage creating on instruments (beautiful sounding instruments, supportive environment, free exploration within structure, and encouragement of teachers who observed and sometimes participated.)

Flohr (1979) studied improvisation behavior of four-, six-, and eight-year-old children using Orff xylophones. Twelve children were asked to improvise in free and guided exploration activities. He found that the characteristics of the children's improvisations changed in relation to the child's chronological age, the older children maintained interest in exploring sound possibilities of a single instrument longer than four-year-olds, tonal orientation and cohesiveness of form increased as the children matured, and young children were able to create musical images of verbal stimuli. Later, Flohr (1981) found that short-term music instruction including instrumental improvisation influenced children's developmental music aptitude as measured by the *Primary Measures of Music Audiation* (Gordon, 1979). The improvisation had a positive influence on the children's scores on the test.

One study of children less than three years of age found that the youngest children's singing forms were floating and resembled scribbled drawings (Dowling, 1988). Dowling's floating spontaneous singing is similar to the motor energy Flohr found in instrumental free explorations. Kratus (1991, 1996) suggested seven levels in learning to improvise. These are: exploration, process-oriented, product-orientated, fluid, structural, stylistic, and personal improvisation. The first three levels are readily applicable to young children. The first, exploration, includes the free exploration already discussed where the child tries out sounds in a loosely structured context. The second, process-oriented improvisation, is characterized by the child creating more cohesive patterns in the improvisation. The third, product-oriented improvisation, includes structural principles such as tonality and meter.

Developmental Sequences—Composition

Although for young children improvisation is the primary mode of creating, a glimpse at the research on composition proves useful in underlining age differences. For example, Kratus (1985) found developmental differences among song compositions of children aged five to thirteen. The five- and six-year-old children did not use formalized endings whereas the seven-year-old children used logical resolutions (endings) to melodic or rhythmic motives.

Tilman and Swanwick (1989) suggested musical creativity involves spiral development. In spiral development a child may gradually progress to more stylized forms of composition or improvisation and then return to use characteristics of earlier development. For example, a child most often improvises music that incorporates four measure phrases characterized by repetition and contrast, but at times returns to the plodding accented durations typical of earlier improvisations (Biasini, Thomas, and Pogonowski, 1970). Tilman and Swanick identified a developmental sequence for instruments and singing based on Piaget's work and characterized by spiral development rather than discrete stages. The **sensory** mode (free exploration) describes three-year-olds' musical behavior. For example, children experiment with the sounds an instrument makes as in free exploration. The **manipulative** mode (motor skills) characterizes four- or five-year-olds. For example, children discover how to produce scales (especially if the instrument is shaped to produce a scale, for example, an Orff xylophone would adapt to production of a scale more easily than a guitar). The **personal** mode (intense personal expression) was first seen to appear in songs of four-year-olds. For example, a child may repeat one word such as "zoo" over and over again with different melodies and pitch ranges. The **vernacular** mode (music conventions of the culture) is characterized by musical cliché, symmetrical phrases, and ostinati. The personal and vernacular modes continue to age nine. The other modes identified by Tilman and Swanick, **speculative, idiomatic, symbolic**, and **systematic** are seen as occurring during ages ten and above (Swanwick and Tilman, 1986).

Structure in Children's Creating

Young children's musical creations often contain structure elements such as repetition, variation, and sequence. Several researchers note that five-year-olds and younger improvise vocal and/or instrumental music that contains structure (Barrett, 1998; Davies, 1992; Dowling, 1988; Flohr, 1979; Moorehead and Pond, 1978; Sundin et al., 1998). For example, Davies studied invented songs of five- and seven-year-olds. She found the vocal compositions to be structurally organized and suggested that the urge to make meaning drives the developmental process. Flohr notated the exploratory instrumental improvisations of twelve subjects. He found half of the four-year-old subjects' (two children) exploratory improvisations exhibited a number of structural elements including melodic repetition, variation, sequence, and inversion (Flohr, 1979, pp. 45–49, 66). What the children are asked to do and the analysis of the children's products help determine the found structure. For example, the structural properties of compositions evaluated with an imposed time limit of ten minutes may be different from composition without a time limit.

Pond's observation of children having their own personal world of sound is an important concept. Adult perceptions of music, including concepts such as form or tonality, may have little to do with the child's world of sound. The environment is also a significant factor in the child's creating. Much of the developmental differences found in children's creating—especially older children—may be influenced by the child's ability to absorb the musical culture that surrounds him or her. For example, when Kalmar and Balasko (1987) observed six-year-olds while creating songs from text rhymes, they often improvised melodies that were similar to songs learned in preschool.

Developmental Milestones for Creating

Milestones in Table 10.4 occur at approximate ages. Individual children exhibit large music skill differences; their skills generally improve with age, experience, and instruction.

Steps to Successful Creating Experiences

Pitfalls to Avoid

Provide the opportunity for exploration of sounds. Thinking of the child's banging on pots, pans, and instruments, as just noise is a mistake. The child is experimenting with sound and her/his creativity will be nurtured in a supportive environment. Be careful with compliments to children three to five years of age. A common behavior for a four-year-old is to stop an activity if an adult interferes or calls attention to the music making.

Table 10.4   Milestones in Creating

MONTHS	MILESTONE
0–24	Exploration of sound-producing objects in the environment.
24	Children are not predisposed to make pretty, symmetrical tunes, but rather patterns, shapes, and structures whose elements are rhythmic figures and intervals (Pond). Improvisations are characterized by plodding and accented durations (pendulum-like regularity) similar to scribbling in art (Flohr).
30	The songs and instrumental improvisations of children less than 3 years have a quality much like scribbles in drawing (Dowling, Flohr).
36–48	Children experiment with their own capacity for sound production with instruments and their own voice.
48	If given the opportunity for free play with instruments and sound-making objects, children will create spontaneous games. They engage in sound exploration, long periods of absorbed activity, unconventional use of instruments, and teaching of peers (Smithrim).
48–60	Improvisations are gradually characterized by melodic repetition, variation, sequence, and inversion. Improvisations are often dominated by the ways a child moves (Cohen). Manipulative mode, personal, and vernacular modes continue past 8 years (Tilman & Swanwick).
72	Songs learned in preschool are used in improvised melodies. More structure leading to decentered perception (attention to overall form rather than attention only to one element [e.g., timbre] at a time).

Steps

- Carefully introduce guided exploration experiences after a child has had ample opportunity to freely explore instruments. Four-year-old children will be helped by ample opportunity to freely explore a wide variety of sound sources followed by guidance from the teacher or parent.
- Use descriptive language to stimulate creating such as "Move like a tree in the wind" or examples in the *Let's Pretend* experiences.
- Do not expect young children to create adult music. Children are not predisposed to make pretty and symmetrical tunes. Their creations are more often patterns, shapes, and structures whose elements are rhythmic figures and intervals. Created songs by children under the age of five have several differences from traditional songs (smaller range, more repetition, chanting and singing, complex rhythms).

Examples of Experiences with Creating Music

Creating music may be encouraged in many ways.

1. *Free exploration (Explore instrument sounds: early childhood years).* Place several instruments in a free play area or construct a sound exploration device such as the *Music House* made of cardboard panels and

containing instruments, props such as shoe boxes, an easel with marking pen, and an audio playback device with headphones (Kenney and Persellin, 2000, pp. 10–13).

2. *Conversations (Improvise on instruments: two to six years).* Teacher and one child or two children may play this game. In conversations two people talk with the instruments. Say to the child, "I'll say something with my instrument and you can answer with your instrument." It is also useful to discuss the idea that talking on the instruments is like talking on the telephone. Provide feedback with statements about the child's productions such as "You played the same rhythm pattern I did and then something different."

3. *Piano play (Improvise on instruments: two to six years).* On a piano, play a pattern on the black keys. For example, play G♭ and D♭ together, move to G♭ and E♭, and then move back to G♭ and D♭. Encourage the child to improvise on the upper part of the piano using the black keys while you play the pattern on the lower keys.

4. *Let's Pretend (Play instrument to show changes in music: three to six years).* This experience is an example of guided exploration. Use an instrument such as a small Orff xylophone or a small keyboard. Begin playing on the instrument and wait for the child to ask to play. Or place the instrument in a play area within the child's reach. Ask the child to pretend she/he is scared or suggest an image. For example, encourage him/her to "Play as if you are scared!" or "Play as if you are a big elephant walking to the water."

5. *Finish the phrase (Improvise on instruments: three to six years).* Demonstrate a short rhythmic or melodic phrase on a drum or xylophone. Then ask the child to finish the phrase with an answer. This game may be done with an adult and child or with two children. In the classroom, each child may find a partner and a space in the room.

6. *Move in a different way (Move to show changes in music: three to six years).* Play a drum or a piece of music and ask each child to move across the room in one way and back in another way. Demonstrate one possibility, for example, skip across the room and tiptoe back. The two movements could show the richness or quantity of the creative thinking. Originality may be observed if the teacher asks everyone to move differently than the other children. Ask the children to show different ways to move to the music.

Summary and Key Points

1. Movement is a concrete mode of learning. Moving to music helps the child internalize music concepts. Young children generally learn more easily through concrete experiences such as movement than with abstract symbolism such as identifying quarter notes of musical notation.

2. The body can perform any musical idea through movement. Any move-
    ment of the body can be transformed into a musical counterpart
    (Dalcroze). Use a wide variety of experiences to reinforce the music-
    movement connection.
3. Expressive movement to music may be creative. A child may imitate
    other children or perhaps seek to follow another in an effort to find the
    correct or socially acceptable movement. Children need a repertoire of
    movements in order to create expressive movements.
4. There are several sources for movement experiences. Many movement
    experiences are available in a wide variety of sources (Burton and Kudo,
    2000; Choksy et al., 2001; Feierabend, 2000a; Sims, 1995; Weikart,
    1998).

Movement and music in early childhood go hand in hand. Children spontaneously
move to recorded and live music. Musically adapted fundamental motor skill milestones are helpful in designing music movement experiences for young children,
including action songs, dance, describing musical movement, expressive movement,
movement with props, movement with sound, movement sequences, singing game
movement, wiggling, tickling, tapping, and word stimuli movement. Experiences
with music and movement should be at the center of young children's music education.

Creating music during the early years may include free exploration, guided exploration, and improvisation. Children require opportunities to experiment with music
for an extended period of time.

1. *Children play, experiment, and create music improvisations.* The task
    of both the teacher and parent is to encourage the child, not get in the
    child's way, and later guide his/her efforts. Child behaviors that occur
    during free play may **not** occurr during teacher-led activities (Smithrim,
    1997). Andress (1980) described several models for sound exploration
    settings including a moveable wall enclosed area (e.g., a refrigerator box)
    with different sound-making sources that can be changed from week
    to week.
2. *Environment is an important element in children's creativity.* As they
    play with sound, children will naturally develop motives and patterns
    from the music that they hear in their home, school, and culture.
    Trollinger (1978) found that families of highly creative women
    attended concerts, other cultural events, and traveled together. Highly
    creative women also began music lessons earlier in life (94 percent by
    the age of six as opposed to 40 percent of the lesser creative). Free
    music exploration has yielded no gender differences (Sundin et al.,
    1998, p. 49). It is difficult to be musically creative in life without musi-
    cal skills. There is some indication that parents who are tolerant and
    allowed independence foster creativity in kindergarten children (Gar-
    ren, 1997).

11

Experiences: Playing Instruments, Reading, and Writing

Children love to play standard musical instruments, instruments designed for young children, and sound-making objects found in the environment. Children will do almost anything–even sit still and patiently wait—to have a chance to play an instrument. Even very young children under six months of age are able to play small instruments such as rattles and small maracas. Instruments belong in the home, the child's classroom music center, and group time.

Instruments

Instruments are often divided into the two main categories of pitched and non-pitched, those that produce a definite pitch such as a piano or guitar and those that produce a sound of indefinite pitch such as a handclap, cymbal, or rattle. MENC (1994c) lists standards for a variety of instruments from different cultures. Playing instruments is related to moving because the playing of instruments requires movement (Chapter 10). For example, playing by using body percussion such as stomp and clap is also a movement experience.

Pitched instruments for young children include tone bells, step bells, Orff instruments, Autoharp, dulcimer, chorded zithers, electronic keyboard, Montessori bells, piano, guitar, violin, voice, recorders, and boom whackers (long colored tubes set to specific pitches). Families of instruments are string, woodwind, brass, and percussion. The families include several instruments for children to identify by sound and sight (three years and above): violin, cello, string bass, flute, clarinet, bassoon, saxophone, trumpet, trombone, horn, tuba, drum, cymbal, and timpani.

Nonpitched instruments for young children to play and identify by sound and sight include rhythm sticks, claves, body percussion (stomp, pat legs, clap, tap, snap), woodblock, cowbell, finger cymbals, triangle, jingle bells, bells, tambourine, castanets (on sticks), sand blocks, shakers (maracas), egg maracas, gong, and drums.

Found sound-making instruments are objects that can be used to produce sound. For example, pots and pans (Richards and Richards, 1974a, 1974b), wood ruler or pencil, straws, cardboard cylinders, newspaper, cups, and balloons.

Developmental Milestones for Playing

The following milestones are set to approximate ages. Individual children exhibit large music skill differences; their skills generally improve with age, experience, and instruction.

Table 11.1　Milestones in Playing Skill Development

MONTHS	MILESTONE
2–5	Simple play with rattle.
4–8	Bangs in play. Interested in sound production.
5–13	Rings bell purposively.
8–17	Pokes piano key with isolated index finger, and listens then pokes another key (Michel and Rohrbacher).
12	Claps hands (pat-a-cake) in imitation of adult. Able to shake small maracas, jingle bells, and rattles. Initiates music play.
18	Enjoys shaking maracas to fast tempi (160+ bpm) (Loong). Will attempt striking many items in the environment—instruments, pots, pans, books, etc. May play with instrument for several minutes.
24	Able to play sticks. Able to strike xylophone and step bells. Child will independently choose and play a musical instrument.
30	Better motor control for playing rhythm instruments. Will be drawn to and will experiment with other instruments such as piano, guitar, or autoharp.
36	Children are capable of playing many percussion instruments, e.g., woodblock, tambourine, claves, guiro, and cowbell. Also able to strum autoharp, dulcimer, and zither. Will respond to call and response task with instruments. Many children start Suzuki violin or piano at 3 years (to start instruction child should have attention skills, interest in instrument, and coordination skills for holding, standing for violin and sitting for piano). Able to control mallets on xylophone.
48	Capable of more control of mallets for xylophone.
60	Guitar instruction is often appropriate.
72	Instruction on violin, piano, and guitar are appropriate for most children (see 36 months for violin and piano; 60 months for guitar). Children are able to take turns with instruments.

Steps to Successful Playing Experiences

Pitfalls to Avoid

Many adults remember a time in their childhood when they wanted to play an instrument, but never had the opportunity. Children often remember for several weeks that they did not get a turn playing in class. Select only those instruments or musical toys that are durable and safe. Maracas can crack and the beans or metal inside can prove dangerous. Instruments such as sticks can injure a child other than the child playing the instrument. When passing out sticks, make sure each child has enough space so that hitting another child is avoided. Choose an instrument appropriate for the size of the child. There are several sizes of violins for children to begin at an early age and in Italy at least one bassoonist is using a small bassoon with children age four years and older. Be careful not to push the child too soon with practice and playing instruments. The child's self-concept and attitude toward music may suffer.

- Involve as many children as possible. Each child should have a turn with the instrument. For children under the age of four use the same instrument (also same in color, shape, size) because the children commonly want what their friends are playing. For example, it is common for a child to say, "I want the red sticks (like her friend)."
- Select high quality instruments; for example, the Parent's Choice Award in 2001 was Bob McGrath's rhythm band set of eight instruments (2001).
- Demonstrate each instrument including how it is held, played, and how to take care of the instrument. For example, maracas should not strike the floor. Encourage children to experiment with different ways to play an instrument, such as at varying degrees of loud and soft, playing short and long, moving up and moving down, even and uneven, or fast and slow.
- Standardize a way to pass out and collect instruments. Ask children to show the appropriate behavior (e.g., sitting quietly) in order to receive an instrument. For collecting instruments try movement like a march around the room and have a box for collecting instruments. As the children march by, they place their instrument in the box. A good idea for mallets and sticks is to have the children put the sticks under their arms as soon as they get them— this keeps them from banging the sticks or mallets around, hitting instruments, and hitting each other.
- Taking turns for six-year-olds usually works well. Take care when asking younger children to wait and take turns. Their concept of time is different from adults and they may not understand waiting until the next class or waiting until it is their turn.

Examples of Experiences with Playing Music

1. *Music play (Explore instrument sounds; birth and above).* Encourage musical play. Play includes exploring and creating (Chapter 10). Play is a natural and important child-centered activity (Custodero, 2002; Morrison, 1998; Tarnowski, 1999); likewise, playing instruments and sound-making objects is also natural for the young child. A child experimenting and exploring an instrument such as a single bell is introduced to the musical concepts of timbre (the timbre or tone color of a bell when struck with different objects), duration (you can ring the bell several times using fast moving durations and slow moving durations), and volume (you can make the sound softer or louder with different mallets) (Andress, 1980, pp. 88–89).

2. *Experiment with xylophone and simple bordun (Playing instruments: two-four years)*. Demonstrate how to **pull** the sound from the xylophone with the mallet rather than striking the xylophone. Proper care of the instruments during the first use is extremely important. Use two xylophones with removable bars (Orff xylophones) and remove the E, G, A, B, and D bars from the xylophones; the parent or teacher plays the bordun by simultaneously playing the F and C bars while the child plays another xylophone. A bordun is usually a uniform bass accompaniment like that of the droning of a bagpipe (F and C played together). By the age of four the child is ready to play the bordun. The bordun can be used with creating experiences from such as *Finish the phrase, Conversations* (p. 115) or as an accompaniment to improvisation.

3. *Making instruments and discriminating sound qualities (Making instruments, listening; two years and above)*. Use found or simple materials for children to make instruments independently or with adults. For tambourines, lace two paper plates together and tie small bells to the edges with yarn. For sandpaper blocks, glue sandpaper to one side of small two-inch wood blocks. For more ideas, see Richards and Richards (1974a, 1974b); Turner and Schiff (1995).

4. *Autoharp play (Playing instruments; three years and above)*. An adult and a child can play the Autoharp and its electronic equivalent, chromaharp, or two older children can begin by playing the Autoharp together. Do not use the Autoharp if it (or any other instrument!) is not in tune. The electronic chromaharp is a better choice if the teacher lacks the skill to tune the Autoharp. Use a song that works with one chord harmony, for example, *Sally Go Round*. While singing the song, the adult and child can divide the two Autoharp tasks of strumming and pressing a chord button (the song only needs the one chord **G** to serve as an accompaniment). After approximately age five, the child can do both tasks. Expand the play with a two-chord song such as *Mary Had a Little Lamb*. Figure 11.1 illustrates where the chords change in respect to the words of the song.

5. *Meet the brass (Recognizing instruments; three years and above)* (expand to meet the strings, woodwinds, percussion). Start introduction of instrument families by the age of three. Two good ways to introduce instruments are to invite performers to visit and to attend a rehearsal or concert. This brass quintet example involves listening and perceiving, interpreting and analyzing sound, synthesizing individual brass sounds into a quintet, and evaluating characteristics of the instruments. Some orchestras expand the idea to *Meet the Orchestra* and include a petting zoo for the instruments where children are able to see, hear, play, and experiment with inexpensive instruments under the supervision of adults.

The Autoharp or electronic equivalent, for example, chromaharp (to avoid tuning the Autoharp) chords are above the word at which point you should strum the instrument.

C   G7   C
Mary had a little lamb, little lamb, little lamb,

C   G7   C
Mary had a little lamb, its fleece was white as snow.

Figure 11.1   Chording to a song

6. *Play the monochord (Playing instruments; three years and above).* Use a Montessori monochord or construct a simple one-string instrument by using a cardboard box with a large rubber band. Demonstrate to the child or children how making the string (rubber band) shorter or longer will change the pitch (higher and lower). Give the child or children an opportunity to experiment with the instrument.

Introduction to Reading and Writing

In learning English, French, or any other language, reading and writing are intertwined. It is the same in learning music—reading music, writing music, and performing music are parts of the process of associating symbols with sounds. Formal reading and writing music often begins in first and second grade. Younger children's experiences are primarily prereading and prewriting experiences. For example, a prereading experience is hearing, clapping, and moving to rhythm patterns that will later be used in reading (e.g., stick notation or dashes and dots). Another prewriting experience is using flat wooden sticks to represent rhythm patterns. Children less than six years of age are able to manipulate music notation. However, there is no reason to believe that reading and writing experiences before six years of age are necessary or desirable. Children taught standard music notation after they receive a substantial prereading base may catch up and surpass children who have learned to read earlier.

Research on Reading and Writing

Issues

How do children learn to read and write? What should be taught first, reading or writing? There are no firm answers to either question. Reading language and reading music represent challenging perceptual tasks for the young child. The process of learning to read and write is not fully understood, but there are principles such as emergent literacy (outlined below) garnered from language research and practice. Reading symbols, or at least the awareness that sounds are related to symbols on the written page, appears to come before writing symbols, but it is possible that some children in composition programs try to write a sound or are able to write a sound before they are able to read any form of musical notation. Although reading music and reading language are different tasks, there are similarities and the vast amount of literature on reading language may help in understanding music reading. Ideas from reading language applied to music include:

1. *Emergent literacy.* Children first learn about reading at home where they acquire emergent reading. Hearing music, exploring instruments, singing, moving to music, and seeing written music in the home sets the stage for learning that the pitches on the page are related to particular sounds.

2. *Intermodal.* Reading is a complex task requiring the child to attend to visual cues, sound cues, and when writing, apply physical coordination skills.

3. *Phonological awareness (spoken words can be decomposed into basic sound units or phonemes).* Children learning to read music need to realize that music can be decomposed into basic sound units of short patterns and notes.

4. *Emergent reading: knowledge of letters—pitches and rhythms.* Children learn pitch names by playing with tone bells (marked with pitch names), hearing singing syllables (e.g., sol, mi, la), and later decoding and sounding out musical symbols. In the same way, children learn rhythm durations and patterns by playing with rhythm instruments, hearing rhythm syllables (e.g., ta, tt, ta), and later decoding and sounding out rhythm syllables.

5. *Two broad approaches.* In language reading two broad approaches are debated. The first, phonics, teaches children letter and sound relationships so they can decode new words by breaking them down into component sounds. The second, whole-language, teaches children to recognize whole words by sight and use the context of the sentence to figure out meaning. The phonics approach is analogous to teaching standard musical notation as quarter notes, eighth notes, and single pitches. The whole-language approach is analogous to teaching standard musical notation as rhythmic and tonal patterns.

Research about Reading Music

In music there is support for a whole-language approach (Gordon, 1997; Upitis, 1992). Experienced music readers are found to read ahead of the music they are performing in units or chunks (Hodges, 1992). Hodges summarizes (1) research shows a high correlation between sight-reading rhythm patterns and sight-reading in general; (2) the advantage of one particular syllabic (e.g., do, re, mi) or mnemonic device (e.g., ta ti-ti) is unclear; (3) tonal pattern instruction is effective; and (4) the advantage of body movement in reading (e.g., hand signs) is unclear.

Research about Writing Music

Several researchers examined children's writing of music and making symbolic representations of music (Bamberger, 1994; Davidson and Colley, 1987; Davidson and Scripp, 1988; Domer and Gromko, 1996; Gromko, 1994; Upitis, 1992). Bamberger found answers to several questions by asking children to listen to a clapped rhythm pattern and then write it down on paper. She found a child's responses could be placed into one of two general types of notation, which she labeled figural and formal (Figure 11.2). By formal she means that the notations in some way indicate how each word or sound relates to the underlying steady beat. In figural the notations show figures or chunks rather than the relationships between sounds (see Figure 11.2). In Bamberger's research a child with prior music training usually responded to the metric or formal aspects of rhythm while a child without prior music training usually responded to the figural aspects of the rhythm. An important element of the research is that children without training will usually respond to the figural aspects of rhythm. After prereading and writing experiences (emergent), the sequence of instruction should move to figural representations rather than to the metrical aspects of rhythm.

Different researchers describe the children's notations in somewhat different ways, but all researchers note progression from scribbles or no representation to counting or units to groupings (metrical or figural) and finally to true metric or standard notation (Domer and Gromko, 1996; Upitis, 1992, p. 48). Gromko (1994) suggests that children may notate pitch before rhythm. Walker (1978, 1981, 1987a, 1987b) notes similarities in the visual representations for sounds. He writes that humans "have an innate mechanism for processing, storing, and transferring across

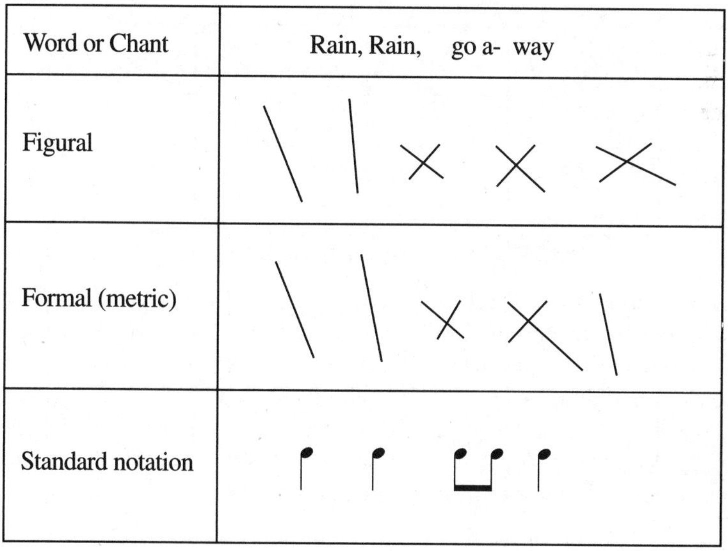

Word or Chant	Rain, Rain, go a- way
Figural	
Formal (metric)	
Standard notation	

Figure 11.2 Figural and formal notation

modalities information relating to auditory movements" (Walker, 1987a, p. 492). He finds children across cultures make up similar symbols to stand for musical sounds, although in one study he finds "Musical training is the most important single factor in choices of visual metaphor for sounds" (Walker, 1987a, p. 500).

Reading and Writing Tools

Several tools are used to help children read and write music. Many of these tools are in the Kodály method since a major goal for the Kodály method is to promote music literacy.

Rhythm—Mnemonics

Teachers often use mnemonics to help teach rhythm, but it is unclear if any particular system is better than another (Hodges, 1992).

For more complex duration and rhythm pattern syllables applicable to older children see (Choksy et al., 2001; Gordon, 1994).

Rhythm—Iconic Representation

Iconic representations are part of most teachers' tools. The representations are used for rhythm, pitch, and musical form although the use of icons is based more on theory (e.g., Bruner) than on research results. See Figure 11.4 for the sequence of icons for "Rain, Rain." The teacher leads the student from representation of the steady beat to realization that the steady beat umbrellas do not match the way the words move.

Duration	Kodály	Gordon	Word	Number
 ♩	ta	du	walk	1
♫	ti ti	du-de	run run	1 and
 ♬	ti-ri-ti-ri- or tika-tika	du-ta-de-ta	Miss-is-sip-pi	1 e and a

Figure 11.3   Examples of mnemonic representations

Representation of the steady beat/pulse	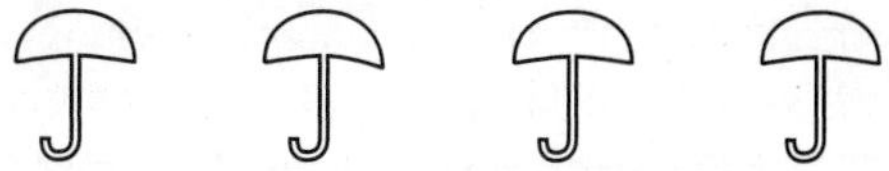
How can we make the picture fit the sound? Split the third umbrella? Oops, we'll get wet!	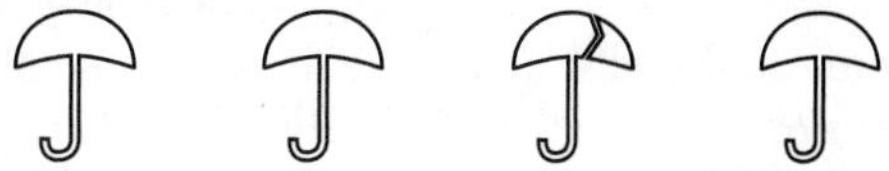
Make two little umbrellas for the third beat.	
The two little umbrellas are holding hands!	
Remove the top and the icon looks similar to standard notation.	
Standard notation.	

Figure 11.4   Iconic representation of *Rain, Rain*

Melody—Hand Signs and Syllables

Use the hand to show young children the contour of pitch. For example, show the up, down, same, stepwise and skipwise movement of the pitches. Two or three hand signs, for example, sol, mi, and la, can be used with four- and five-year-olds. See Figure 6.3 for pictures of hand signs.

Taxonomies

Taxonomies are used for reading and writing sequences. For example rhythm durations are listed in order of presentation beginning with quarter, two eighths, quarter rest, half, and six eights in 6/8 meter. The next five duration elements are dotted quarter-eighth, two dotted quarters in 6/8 meter, syncopation, eighth-dotted quarter, and quarter eighth in 6/8 meter (Choksy et al., 2001, p. 93). Choksy lists melodic patterns beginning with sol, mi and then adding la, re and do. The five pitches (do, re, mi, sol, and la) form a pentatonic scale. A standard progression of pitches on a staff is (1) iconic representation (no staff), (2) one-line staff notation, (3) two-line staff notation,

(4) three- to five-line or standard staff notation. Rhythm and tonal patterns are also sequenced (see Chapter 7, taxonomies) (Choksy et al., 2001; Gordon, 1994).

Developmental Milestones for Reading and Writing

The milestones in Table 11.2 are set to approximate ages. Individual children exhibit large music skill differences; their skills generally improve with age, experience, and instruction.

Table 11.2 Milestones in Reading and Writing Music

MONTHS	MILESTONE
0–60	Children require musical experiences and training to prepare them for music reading. Hearing and seeing music in the home is an important part of emergent literacy (language research).
< 60	Children have been shown to be able to manipulate music notation before the age of 5. Use of figural or iconic notation is common. Children without music training respond to figural aspects of rhythm (Bamberger). Reading and writing often accompany the experience of learning to play the violin or piano.
72	Children are able to recognize distinctive visual features of letters and are ready to identify visual features of quarter note, eighth note (2 barred together), quarter rest, and pitch notation on 2-3 lines. Able to use sticks to notate four-beat measures comprised of eighth and quarter notes. Able to use two-line notation to notate two pitches. After 6 years children can gradually add more to their reading and writing symbols including: more rhythm patterns, half note, eighth note standing alone, dotted notes; syncopation, sixteenths, sixteenth and eighth patterns, triple meter, 6/8 meter, compound meters, pitches, tonal patterns (sequence is important). For example, 6 to 7-year-olds will not be able to read and write half and quarter notes if they have not studied steady beat earlier).

Steps to Successful Reading and Writing Experiences

Pitfalls to Avoid

The chief pitfall to avoid is failing to provide ample emergent music reading experiences.

Steps

- Provide a firm foundation for reading and writing with many experiences in music. Include a wide variety of music. If the objective is to enable children to read quarter, eighth, and half notes by second grade, provide early experiences in moving, playing, singing, listening, and creating that use those rhythm durations.
- Sound before symbol. Provide prereading experiences. Include sound exploration, rhythm and tonal instruments for play, storybooks with music,

examples of music notation, and—if at all possible—parent or other adult models of doing, reading, and writing music.

- Allow children to discover notation on their own with gentle teacher questions rather than telling them how to notate. Children often exhibit their own creative ways to notate rhythms (Bamberger, 1994; Walker, 1978, 1981, 1987a). For example, play a short rhythm pattern and ask the children to draw what they hear with crayons/pencils and paper.
- After prereading experiences, use pictures (Figure 11.4).
- Provide motivation to learn to read and write. For example, ask the child to help you write out their composed music so that they can remember it for next week. There is no research base about how early music reading and writing might aid future development.
- Provide experiences with rhythm and tonal patterns. For example, use felt boards or manufactured erasable slates for the notation of rhythm and melody.

Examples of Reading and Writing Experiences

1. *Show the rhythm with manipulatives (Prereading, stick notation; four years and above).*
   The use of manipulative aids is common in classrooms. For example, wooden sticks or writing materials such as erasable white/black boards, old newspapers, and crayons can be used for notating rhythm. Give each child a set of twelve flat wooden sticks. Play four steady beats on the drum and ask the children to use the sticks to show the rhythm. Be sure to give them the freedom to show the way they want to represent the music. For example, a child may place two sticks close together to show how they are shorter durations or that they move faster in relation to the steady beat. Later, you should demonstrate how the standard music stick notation represents the rhythm pattern.

2. *Stories about So-mi (Sing pitches accurately and in tune; three years and above).*
   A set of stories about a little boy named So-mi provides emergent reading experiences. Teachers and parents read stories to children and the children, teachers, and parents can sing the hero's name and make other sounds present in the stories (Manins, 1987). The stories help children learn about reading through emergent reading experiences of hearing music, singing, and seeing written music.

3. *Two-line notation (Writing music; five years and above).*
   After working with the figural notation for "Rain, Rain" (Figure 11.4), ask the children to move their arms up and down to show the pitch movement. On a two-line staff place note heads on the lines to represent pitch movement (Figure 11.5). The two-line staff is a simplification of the standard five-line music staff.

Summary and Key Points

Many musical instruments are appropriate for young children and the opportunity to engage in free play with the instruments and sound-making objects should be available.

1. Start early in infancy with small instruments such as rattles.
2. Give children ample opportunity to explore and play with all sound-making objects.
3. Encourage their explorations, improvisations, and creations.
4. Compare and contrast the sounds of different instruments. Encourage all young children not only to explore instruments but also to play the instrument, listen, and play and listen again. The approach of Montessori (Chapters 2 and 6) exemplifies careful listening and teacher questions leading to discovery.

Reading and writing music represent challenging perceptual tasks for the young child. Experiences for young children less than six years of age are primarily prereading and prewriting experiences.

1. Sound before symbol. Children need experience with creating, performing and listening to music before reading or writing music notation.
2. Findings from language research such as emergent literacy and phonological awareness apply to music. Children first learn about reading at home where they acquire emergent reading: hearing music and seeing written music in the home set the stage for learning that the pitches on the page are related to particular sounds.
3. After many prereading experiences, start reading/writing instruction with figural representations.

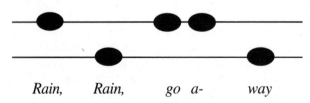

Rain,   Rain,   go a-   way

Figure 11.5   Two line notation of pitch movement in *Rain, Rain*